FUGITIVE PAPERS

FUGITIVE PAPERS

OF

RUSSELL GORDON SMITH

WITH A FOREWORD BY

FRANKLIN HENRY GIDDINGS

AND AN INTRODUCTION BY

HERBERT EDWIN HAWKES

Essay Index Reprint Series

BOOKS FOR LIBRARIES PRESS
FREEPORT, NEW YORK

LIBRARY OF CONGRESS CATALOG CARD NUMBER:

68-22947

PRINTED IN THE UNITED STATES OF AMERICA

TO THOSE STUDENTS OF
COLUMBIA COLLEGE
WHO CAME INTO CONTACT
WITH HIM

FOREWORD

We called him "Bus" as a nickname of endearment. It had been his attempt to say "Russell" when learning to talk. Our most constant reaction to him was affection. Next to this feeling and not appreciably inferior to it was something like respectful wonder at his quality and his gifts. Without analyzing them we knew them for more than talent. They were always flashing upon us in unpredictable ways, which lit up our duller insights and slower understandings. We talked of genius, but what we meant by the word we did not know. Will anybody ever know?

But we knew some things that we could always count on finding in Smith's character and in his mind. On the scientific side his intellect was a steel trap. It clicked. Its accuracy was uncanny. Yet he knew the limitations of science; what it is and what it is not. He knew where knowledge begins and ends, and it did not suffice him. Beyond knowledge lie the infinite and eternal mysteries, and before these he was the reverent but never the mystical philosopher who fools himself with meaningless phrases. Smith was content to look into the unknown with agnostic humility and let it go at that. To beauty his sensitiveness was exquisite. Poetry and art were the substance of his life, and for felicity of expression he had unbounded regard. What was worth saying was worth

[vii]

saying in a beautiful way, which to him meant an illuminating way, and at any cost a simple, accurate, unpretentious way.

His courage was great, his fortitude unfailing. When America went into the World War, Smith was among the first to volunteer. Assigned to duty in a southern camp and hospital, prostrated by influenza, he was stricken. From the initial attack he recovered only to go down quickly to apparently inevitable death from tuberculosis. Officers, nurses, and medical experts reported that he was doomed. Then a devoted mother took him in hand. She nursed him back to life and a semblance of health.

The years that followed brought a succession of torturing operations, with months now and then of respite. Mind and soul grew though body faltered. Painfully he wrote when strength permitted. With heroic will he returned to Columbia University to resume candidacy for the doctor's degree.

An instructor was wanted in Columbia College to give undergraduates a foundation course in sociology. Smith was persuaded to undertake it.

Then came amazing revelation of his intellectual and spiritual power. He met a restless assemblage of young men, curious as to what they were in his lecture room for. Instantaneously (no other word applies) he "got" them, thrilled them, and held them. At the end of the hour they did not know what had happened to them except that they meant never to lose any word that he should have to offer them. In a few days their homage had become devotion. And yet they knew and claimed

him as one of themselves. They understood such a relationship in athletic affairs; compelling experience of it
in the classroom was new.

The outpouring of vitality which went into that teaching would have drained a strong constitution. To Smith
it was fatal. A succession of warning breakdowns, and
presently operations more dreadful than those which had
come before, precluded hope that routine work could
ever be resumed.

When the end came it was believed that more than
an extraordinary life had gone out in night. A partially
fulfilled promise would be remembered for a time and
then forgotten as music of the virtuoso who has left no
compositions. We knew of the weary hours which he
had given to writing but supposed that his manuscripts
were little more than drafts of chapters of a sociological
treatise, destined never to be completed. That he had left
also an enduring record of his marvelous talks with his
boys, and that it was alive as his talks were with "beauty,
laughter, and love," with illuminating knowledge and
with sane philosophy, could not then have been believed. Yet here it is.

Probably the pages were sketched from day to day
before meeting students, but certainly they were after-
wards worked over with all that sensitive feeling for
word and phrase which made his sentences so nearly
perfect, never pretentious, or labored, but simple, truth-
ful, and right. As I have read them, I have felt the
gratitude of one who loved him, that "Bus" as an inspiration and a teacher is not dead and will not die
for generations to come. The mind which was genius,

FOREWORD

the soul which was beauty, laughter, love, and fortitude, live and will go on living.

I have let myself go in expression of feeling. I could not do otherwise. But now let me try as a lifelong student of the subject to which my comrade and quondam pupil also was devoted, to set down a judgment. This book is the best introduction to sociology that has ever been written. Fortunate will be the college boy or girl into whose hands it falls before wits have been addled by confusion worse confounded, or antagonized by stupidity. It is not a treatise, an exposition. It is a perception, an insight. It awakens, it drives. It makes clear what sociology is, and reveals its value, for thought and for life, for discrimination, for appraisal, for fulfillment of the Miltonic injunction: "Nor love thy life nor hate, but what thou livest live well."

FRANKLIN HENRY GIDDINGS

COLUMBIA UNIVERSITY
IN THE CITY OF NEW YORK
May, 1930

CONTENTS

INTRODUCTION

This little volume is published in the hope that it may preserve for those who knew him at least a suggestion of the spirit and mind of a much loved and much admired man. Probably no one came into an intimate understanding of him to the same extent as his students, to whom he gave himself without stint. And no teacher in Columbia College during the past twenty years has gained and held such an influence—an influence almost hypnotic in its character—over the students in his classes. His powers of analysis, his almost uncanny feeling for trenchant phrase, the contrast between his frail body and his vigorous spirit, his struggle for life against hopeless odds, all combine to leave an impression that time cannot efface in the memories of those who knew him. Such spirits are rare, and nothing that will keep that spirit fresh in the minds of his students and possibly give to those who never came under his magic spell some idea of his quality should be neglected.

The Blessed Trinity that he loved to worship—Beauty, Laughter, and Love—may be worthy, but he himself in his own person as well as in his philosophy placed fortitude above them all. "I make this my valedictory: that it matters little whether you retain in memory the facts and theories with which we have perhaps merely bemused ourselves these many weary months; it matters

INTRODUCTION

only that through worship of the aforementioned Blessed Trinity you keep burning always at white heat the living fire of fortitude. For when that goes out, the rest is madness—just plain, stark madness, in the darkness of which there is no beauty and no laughter and no love."

HERBERT EDWIN HAWKES

COLUMBIA UNIVERSITY
IN THE CITY OF NEW YORK
May, 1930

FUGITIVE PAPERS

THE PHILOSOPHY OF A FOOL

And God saw everything that he had made and, behold, it was very bad. On the seventh day, therefore, God could not rest. In the morning and the evening He busied Himself with terrible and beautiful concoctions and in the twilight of the seventh day He finished that which is of more import than the beasts of the earth and the fish of the sea and the lights of the firmament. And he called it Imagination because it was made in His own image; and those unto whom it is given shall see God.

For beauty and divinity are one, and all which partakes of loveliness is divine. But, save in fleeting moments of revealing ecstasy, we see darkly, through the mists of our senses, forgetting that for no other reason was imagination given unto us than that we might refashion the Creator's wretched handiwork, that we might remake an ugly universe in the likeness of our dreams.

And this is the first principle of the philosophy of a fool; that it matters little whether a thing be true or good or useful; it matters only that it be beautiful. It is true that the dog belongs to the phylum Vertebrata,

[3]

to the class Mammalia, to the family Canidae, to the genus Canis; but it is beautiful that Pericles, sleeping there in the amber firelight, is a Dravidian priest reincarnate who holds within his shaggy head the wisdom of a thousand unrecorded years. Miss Minnie Hardface was a good woman and swerved not by a kiss-breadth or a wink-length from the Ten Commandments. This is incontrovertible, for it is implicit in the inscription on the austere slab which marks the abiding place of her virtuous fragments. Mary, of the brown hair and red lips, was bad, and because she was lifted by moonlight to the threshold of divinity, they killed her with cool bows and cold shoulders. But white-faced clematis makes a virgin's bower of Mary's grave; while stinkweed sprouts from the soil that covers Minnie Hardface. Flowers are discriminating.

It is useful to make money and to save it; to be self-controlled and law-abiding and respectable. Useful are the factories where blear-eyed women and cadaverous men sweat and groan and stink; useful are cacophonous machines and fusty libraries and the misshapen piles of clay and stone wherein pig-faced men chant raucous litanies to the God of Gold and perform the filthy liturgies of lust. All these things are useful—and hideous.

And useless is the color of the moon's dawning; and the awful majesty of mountains before sunrise; and the harlequin opal of the evening sky; and the tinkle of white rain among the young green leaves of maples; and the spume of a turquoise sea heaving beneath wind-tormented clouds; and a crescent moon above the autumnal ghost of an elm; and the tawny hair of a child against a dark and ancient tapestry; and the faint incense of Jacqueminot from the body of an adored woman. All these things are useless—and beautiful. But a fool has no choice.

There is a world beyond common-sense and common-sensation and its invisible frontiers are impassable barriers to all who are reasonable and practical and respectable. Only those can cross its borders who have been initiated into the mysteries of the seventh day of creation. For in this world beyond sense and sensation, folly is wisdom, failure is success, wealth is poverty, truth is a lie, and the greatest economy is to throw away all useful things. And by the fantastic standards of this wonderland nothing matters at all save laughter, beauty, and love—these three, Blessed Trinity, one and inseparable.

CHRISTMAS, 1917

Permit me in closing tonight to indulge for a moment in the luxury of a digression. In a sense it is not a digression at all, for ceremonials, festivals, and celebrations are rightfully of the subject matter of Sociology; and it is about Christmas that I want to speak—Christmas, 1917.

For us Americans there is in the Christmas of 1917 a strange paradox. Christmas is peculiarly a German festival; and Germany is our bitterest enemy. Christmas is the celebration of the nativity of the Prince of Peace; and the world is a darkling plain where furious armies clash by night. For the whole human race, indeed, there has been no Christmas like the one which lies before us. How shall we observe it—with what emotions, with what beliefs, with what hopes? "Merry" is the proverbial modifier of Christmas; can we use it now without a blush of shame? "Peace on Earth" is the theme of Christmas songs. Can we sing them without a sneer? "Glory to God" is the paean of Yuletide prayer. Can we offer it without the bitter consciousness of its futility and mockery?

On the sixth day of December in the harbor of Hali-

[6]

fax the French munition transport Mont Blanc collided with a Belgian relief ship. Within ten minutes the peaceful little Canadian village was a bloody 'shambles of mutilated women and children, a smoking hell of ruined homes. Little babies lay naked in the frozen streets, their tender bodies torn to crimson shreds by flying timber and broken glass. Mothers groped about in the débris screaming, not with their own pain but with the agony of losing all they loved. Men went insane from horror. The big throbbing heart of America was touched, and relief trains dashed to the scene of disaster, carrying comfort and salvation. Then what happened? A blinding, stinging blizzard grumbled up from the Atlantic, delaying the willing aid and crushing out hundreds of human lives in darkness and suffering. In contracts, bills of lading and other legal instruments this harrowing catastrophe would be called an "act of God."

For three years—and more—the tragedy of Halifax has been equaled and surpassed in gruesomeness and wanton slaughter on the plains of Flanders, in Northern France, in Serbia and Armenia. The world has grown gray and old with suffering. Human life has been squandered with the riotous prodigality of an angry child amid Dresden china. Human hearts have been torn with anguish till our sensibilities no longer react to the glaring headlines of the daily press. In the awful silence between the thunder of vandal guns we have lifted up our eyes unto the hills, and there has been no answer save the echo of our wailing cry.

It would seem that we must needs revaluate our ethical and social values; find another moral basis for life; formulate a new religion; create a new God. In what image shall we carve him? We can no longer reconcile omnipotence with divine mercy. Confronted by a million ghastly tragedies of death and destruction, the human mind is logically compelled to denounce an all-powerful God as a brutal fiend whose touch would desecrate a gallows. That divine omnipotence and divine mercy may transcend the grasp of the finite mind is beside the point. In the only language that we know, founded upon the only sensuous apparatus we have, we must ascribe the horrors about us—if an anthropomorphic interpretation is permissible at all—to the authorship of a power that is either stupid or unscrupulous. The conclusion of H. G. Wells on this point is unavoidable.

What, then, are the attributes of the human deity which reason compels us to postulate? After two thousand years of blundering, of vain groping for an ideal system of social relationships, for a philosophy based upon the unalterable attributes of the human heart, we again turn our faces towards Golgotha, seeing there not the futile martyrdom of a dreamer, but the death of a

[8]

noble radical who builded better than he knew. Science and philosophy, after years of research and experimentation, have established the soundness and practicality of the fundamental dogmas of the Man of Galilee. With Bernard Shaw, we are beginning to ask, "Why not give Christianity a trial?" And this question cannot be answered by those who call themselves Christians, for they know least about it. Christians are the strongest arguments against Christianity. It can be answered by the men going "over the top," battling against barbarism with blood and iron, not less than with loyalty and love, that the kingdom of heaven may be established upon the Earth.

And so it seems to me that we rightfully celebrate Christmas of 1917. It seems to me that the bells should peal the rhythm of rejoicing. For autocracy and tyranny are beaten. Democracies move slowly, but, once started, not all the power of Potsdam and of hell can stay their giant strength. The Italian reverses, the U-boat destruction, the Russian Débâcle are but trivial incidents compared to the splendid certainty that rings in the thunder of Haig's guns, in the songs of the French legions, and in the triumphant hymn of a new Americanism born of the loathing for atrocity and tyranny and dedicated to the high resolve that democracy shall not perish from the earth.

Upon this assigned anniversary of the birthday of

the Man of Sorrows we can, I think, without doing violence to our intelligence, sing glory to a new God carved from the substance of our suffering. And though the darkness now seems deep I think we can already see over the hills of tomorrow the faint streaks of dawn —of peace on Earth, good will towards men.

"Merry" would convey the implication of irreverence, the intimation of an inexcusable levity.

I wish you all a hopeful Christmas and a very happy New Year.

THIS UNIVERSE OF INFINITE COMPLEXITY

More than two thousand years ago a Greek philosopher, with viewpoint remarkably modern, expressed in striking metaphor the fundamental aspect of the world which lies about us. "This world," said Heraclitus, "the one for all, neither one of the gods nor of the human race hath made, but it ever was, and is, and shall be an externally living fire." The flux and fluidity of flame, its inseparability, its intricate interrelationship, its continual metamorphosis, seems indeed a most appropriate rhetorical figure in which to resume that differentiated unity of the sensory world, that essential transitoriness of all things, which has become at once the fundamental postulate of both science and philosophy.

Ceaselessly changing order, orderly ceaseless change, and this everywhere, from the stars to the mud beneath our feet—birth, growth, death, decay, metamorphosis, and resurrection—in a word, evolution, in nature, inorganic and organic, in individual and social life, this is the keynote of the universe into which we are thrust by the accident of birth; to which, through trial and error, we struggle to adjust ourselves; and which,

[11]

throughout the brief span of our existence, we endeavor to understand.

Facing this universe of infinite complexity, men, at various times and in various moods, ask many questions, follow many intellectual and emotional paths, arrive at strangely unlike conclusions. The metaphysician breaks the fetters of sensory impression and on the far side of matter finds what he calls truth. The religionist, seeking the ultimate reality transcending experience, finds it at the other end of prayer and reverently names it truth. The artist, reflecting nature through the prism of his personality, believes in the reality of his concretized dreams and says that his truth is the truth. To the world-old question "What is Truth?" there is no one answer. There are many answers, as many answers as there are moods of the human spirit.

There is a mood of the human spirit in which the mind, focusing its attention upon the communicable and verifiable things of the world, upon the things perceptible to the human senses, and only these, seeks, through clear-sightedness, accuracy, and constructive skepticism, to describe in unambiguous terms the identities, diversities, sequences, and correlations of the material universe and to state the natural laws which underlie it. This is the scientific mood. It does not imply that other moods are fatuous or futile; it does not hold that the truths it enables men to discover are the only truths. Science never has had, never could have had, never will have, any quarrel with Religion, Philosophy, or Art. These begin where it leaves off. It takes experimental facts as "given" and asks no questions about the *Ding an sich*. It seeks to describe as simply and clearly as possible the impressions which the phenomenal world makes upon normal human senses; to summate these impressions in descriptive formulae, or laws; to understand secondary and effective, not final, causes; to describe how things came to be what they now are. It attains these ends through observation, measurement, and classification, through logic, experimentation, and the methods of statistics—methods which, though more or less arbitrary and empirical, seem best adapted to the subject matter. The justification of this type of intellectual activity lies in its expressed or implied purpose to aid man in the rational control of the forces upon which his existence and progress depend. That it has thus justified itself in the past and will probably continue to do so in the future, none can deny.

Nothing could be farther from the truth, however, than the tendency in certain little groups of serious thinkers to believe that because science has described the world in clear-cut terminology, because it has enabled man in some measure to utilize and direct natural forces to his needs and ideals, it has therefore "explained" the universe. The function of science is not explanatory but descriptive. All the physical and chemical facts, theories, and laws, from the guesses of Empedocles to those of Einstein, cannot tell us *why* an electric current passed through water will produce hydrogen and oxygen in the ratio two to one. They can only tell us *how*. Science explains nothing. It cannot answer the questions of a child of six. It can only reduce to simpler and more concise terms our crude description of phenomena which, in the last analysis, are perhaps inexplicable. It can only, as some have put it, organize our common sense. Contrary to a popular conception, the scientist does not pirouette in fiendish glee through the graveyard of romance and sentiment and illusion. He knows too well that behind the symbols of mathematics and the formulae of chemistry and physics and the rigid generalizations of psychology and social science lie the unexplained mysteries of twilight and music, of autumn nights fringed with silver, of human fortitude and idealism. Science has not robbed life of its adventure, nor us of our faith in life's possibilities. It has limited its field, rigidly defined its terms, definitely stated its postulates, arbitrarily selected its standards of truth. Further than this it does not seek to go.

But going even this far, there are almost insuperable difficulties. The scientist seeks to describe that which is forever changing, never static, in categories that are of necessity both static and fixed. His most precise and valid generalizations are, therefore, in a sense, deliberate misrepresentations of the phenomenal world. Did any of you ever see the species *Homo sapiens?* Or bodies attracting one another directly as their masses and inversely as the squares of their distances? Moreover, the scientist is forced by the limitations of mind to make abstractions, imagined separations, of things that are ultimately inseparable. For a fact, a thing, a person, indeed, is only an arbitrary point in an infinite and indivisible sequence. The life history of the tiniest amoeba taken from the scum of a brackish pond would carry us back to the tattered fringes of a nebulous world. Every flower that blows holds within its perfumed chalice the mysteries of birth and dreams. And a complete statement of how this watch was made and how it came into my possession would constitute a textbook of the science of economics.

Sociology is one of the manifestations of the mood I have described as scientific. It is a science, and shares the problems and difficulties of all science. It is a general science, combining the conclusions and laws of the special social sciences into generalizations of universal validity. Its subject matter is human behavior, in its collective aspects, which it attempts to describe and factorize by analytical and statistical methods.

Economics is a special social science, subordinate to sociology, limiting its inquiries to a certain definite complex of social activities. Enough has been said, I hope, about the nature of science in general to forewarn us against the danger of seeking final explanations, final causes, final solutions of social problems in a realm where there is no finality, where each day's inevitable sun drops its gold upon the ashes of burned-out theories and dogmas, where what now is truth, tomorrow will become a fairy tale wherewith to still the cries of fretful children. The scientific seeker after truth realizes that his greatest contribution is not in absolutes but in relatives, that all his skill lies in enlightening the darkness of the path that others after him will tread. We must acquire the intellectual and moral courage to face a world in which nothing is final; in which everything is relative. Dogmatism is cowardice; absolutism an intellectual yellow streak. The scientific study of the economic process will not enable us with assurance and self-confidence to shatter the social clay to bits and then remold it closer to our heart's desire. It will not give us any unalterable convictions about labor and capital, production and distribution, socialism and syndicalism. It should give us an organized body of knowledge, a scientific viewpoint, and the basis for intelligent opinions in current issues. These, properly used, should make for the most effective and worth-while leadership in the social economic life of our generation.

THE NOBLE ANIMAL

In the first semester of this course we exposed our selves to the malignancy of the Evil Eye by daring to ask the prodigious question: How has human society come to be as it now is? or, better, perhaps, How did human societies get this way? If the provisional answer to that question seemed pathetically inadequate, we may find solace, as we have before, in the thought that omniscience is vouchsafed only to God. Our general conclusion was that cultural traits, complexes, and patterns, or in other words, folkways, mores, customs, manners, and usages, owe their present form and content, their complexity and magnitude, to a selectively cumulative process in which the accidents of invention, convergence, and diffusion combine and integrate within limits set by the original nature of man and by the nature of this little planet on which God, in His unerring perspicacity, ordained that man should live. One should, as Mr. Cabell has suggested, avoid anthropomorphology, but you may, if you wish, picture this complicated process of culture-building by imagining the Ironic Artificer of human destiny, sitting aloft on his golden throne, selecting now a culture element here, and now one there, and again

one from over yonder, and so on ad infinitum, and ty-
ing them together into complexes which benighted humans will inevitably regard as rational and beneficent
no matter how illogical and handicapping they may in
reality be. But please do not misinterpret this highly
condensed summary of a process which could be satis-
factorily described only in several bulky volumes. When
I speak of the "accidents" of invention, convergence, and
diffusion I do not for a moment mean to imply that the
making of civilizations is, by any process, "uncaused."
Quite the contrary. I mean that any particular integration of customs and usages, that is, any particular cultural complex is, for the most part, the result of the
fortuitous coming together of independent causal series.
And I would not leave you with the impression that
"historical accident" in this sense is the only way in
which we can explain cultural forms, group habits. I
would not dare thus ignore the awful majesty of the
Eighteenth Amendment which sprang full-grown from
the minds of the Anti-Saloon Leaguers and was therefore necessarily a rational adjustment of human needs
and desires to the life conditions. Our general conclusion about how human societies get this way may be
elaborated somewhat as follows: Through trial and error
over a vast period of at least three hundred thousand
years the social order has been evolved through the in-
teraction of man's primal needs and desires with the

external conditions of human life. This process is psychologically largely a matter of unconscious like response to stimulation, the emotional response, the "religious thrill," predominating and largely controlling, certainly in the earlier stages of social development. These unconscious like responses become stereotyped in folkways which through rational and quasi-rational sanctions develop into mores out of which come all our laws and institutions. Throughout the history of civilization the mores have changed little by rational direction, by purposive control. Changes in the fundamental mores have been brought about usually by social contact, imitation, and borrowing, in a word, by diffusion, and by changes in the material conditions of human life, that is, by the inventions and discoveries of the physical scientists. When Abraham Lincoln wrote the Emancipation Proclamation he changed nothing but the virginal whiteness of the paper on which he wrote. When James Watt invented the double-acting steam engine he laid the corner stone of a new social structure.

Our problem in this semester is, I think, more fascinating and certainly more baffling. To its solving we must bring an even greater measure of scientific caution and impartiality and objectivity. For we are going to ask, and answer as best we can in the light of present knowledge, How is the heritage of the past impressed upon each new generation and how do personalities emerge from specific cultural situations? Which, translated into the vernacular of Columbia College, means: How did you get this way?

Not so many years ago you came into the world a polymorphous-perverse little ape with a billion years of biological evolution precipitated, so to speak, in your dimpled organism. You came naked, without shame, without language, food habits, or manual dexterity; without artistic appreciation, scientific standards, moral ideas, or religious faith; without respect for law and order and with no discernible admiration for Mr. Herbert Hoover. You came with no higher desires than to have your capacious belly filled with milk and your somatic and visceral itches scratched by loving hands.

Now you are sophisticated and supercilious juniors and seniors of Columbia College, weary young intellectuals in a decadent era, murmuring over this, that, and the other in your daily routine, "What a beastly bore!" You are clothed in choicest fabrics and adorned with the totemic symbols of your respective fraternities. You speak and write the English language—fairly well; and you know better than to eat pie with a knife, at least in public. Some of you can probably play eighteen holes of golf in less than a hundred strokes; some of you can lie beautifully to that effect. Some of you think you know what da Vinci tried to convey by the smile of Mona Lisa. Your desires have multiplied; so have your doubts and fears. You still have somatic and visceral itches, but your scratching technique has, I trust, become much more complicated and effective. Think of yourself as a bawling and puking brat with your nose and bladder in perennial flux, and then look at yourself now. *Mirabile visu!* Isn't Nature wonderful? How did you get this way? That's the first question we shall try to answer.

To answer it realistically we shall have to face facts that are pleasant and, more frequently perhaps, facts that are unpleasant. We must at the outset purge ourselves of prudishness and of pruriency. The shudders of Puritanism and the snickers of obscenity will both be tabooed in this course. We shall seek to understand, scientifically if possible, the process of socialization—the social making of human personality. Man is a noble animal—yes, God's most marvelous handiwork. He has idealism and fortitude, and he will lay down his life for a friend. But he has also nutritional, excretory, and, I'm very sorry to say, sexual functions. These functions and their conditionings are ineradicable factors in character, temperament, disposition, and culturized behavior. We shall not ignore these functions, as so many tender-minded sociologists have done in the past, but shall deal with them as frankly as with the so-called higher functions. We shall hold with Plautus, one of the first great humanists: *Homo sum; nihil humani mihi alienum*

THE NOBLE ANIMAL

puto: I am a man; all that concerns my fellow-man is my concern. And that, as Aldous Huxley might phrase it, will probably include both lyric poetry and abnormal eroticism.

THE INDIVIDUAL AND SOCIETY

> Beyond your mind and flesh and blood
> Nothing there is to live or do;
> There is no man, there is no God,
> There is not anything but you.

Thus sang Giovanetti, the anarchist, in his cell in a Federal prison, and for the most part expressed poetically the exact opposite of scientific truth. For beyond your flesh and blood are ten million years of biological evolution, ten million years of adaptations, survivals, and selections, ten million years during which the germinal bases of your essential self have been slowly and inexorably fashioned. And beyond your mind— that baffling complex of sensations, perceptions, emotions, feelings, that mysterious unity of wishing, aiming, purposing, resisting, striving, competing, which some psychologists still vaguely name the ego, is an incredibly vast and complicated and ancient social heritage from which practically the entire content of your mind has been unconsciously derived.

Short of very careful scrutiny and a rather painful kind of self-analysis and introspection, nothing seems so certain as the uniqueness and individuality and independence of our own thoughts and feelings and desires and preferences. But let us look into this matter more critically and concretely. Ask anyone to tell you what he knows about himself, and he will begin to tell you how he differs from Jack and Henry and Bill; he will compare himself in this trait to A, and in that to B; he will express affection for Mrs. X and contempt for Mr. Y; he will tell you that he detests Mary because she raves over Monte Blue, and that he is crazy about Helen because, well, because somehow Helen's eyes are not eyes at all, but deep places full of something shadowy and dank and wholly sweet like violets at night (and incidentally he probably stole that thought from someone else). In short, he cannot talk about himself without talking of others; he cannot think of himself without thinking of others. His most elementary conception of himself is a product of his social contacts and experiences.

Pass from the realm of self-consciousness to the realm of individual behavior and what do you find? You will, if you are intellectually honest, realize very quickly that nine-tenths of all you do or say or think or feel from the time you get up in the morning until the time you go to bed at night is done and said and thought and felt, not in independent self-expression, but in un-critical, unconscious conformity with rules, regulations, group habits, standards, codes, styles, and sanctions that

[24]

were in existence long before you were born. You wear clothes of a certain cut not because your individuality impels you to, but because that cut is in style. You take off your hat to a lady of your acquaintance, not because your ego demands it, but because the social code prescribes it—because you know what's wrong in the picture. You praise this man and denounce that one; you like this man and dislike that one; you accept this article of religious faith and reject that—and, if you think about these evaluations and preferences, you will be forced to the conclusion that practically all your standards and criteria have been socially created.

The further we carry this sort of an analysis the more difficult it becomes to define and isolate that individuality of which we are so often prone to boast. Eventually we have to admit that we are the victims, or the beneficiaries if you prefer, of a gigantic Something which we name Society. The reality of this huge something is undeniable—and yet, just what is it?

PARENTHESIS

Several times in this course you have heard me say
that data were lacking for the final solution of the
particular problem under discussion. You have won-
dered perhaps—especially those of you whose interest
in the course centers primarily around the three points
of academic credit—why I discuss subjects that cannot
be reduced to memorizable formulae. I want to take a
minute or two to tell you why.

When I took my oral examination for that Teutonic
atavism called Ph.D., I had acquired laryngeal dexterity
with the fifty-seven systems of sociology and the hundred and fifty-seven theories of society then in vogue.
I could drool glibly about what Spencer and Comte and
Giddings and Ward and Durkheim and Tarde and De
Greef and Who's-it thought they thought about collective behavior. In my wisdom I rejoiced and was ex-
ceeding glad—for a while. Then I stepped out, so to
speak, in quest of this thing I was supposed to understand—this thing named human life, human society. I
got in with the organized uplifters and monkeyed
around in the slums. I consorted with doctors and nurses,
and saw life, with bleeding lips and tired eyes, sitting in

[26]

the clinics and hospitals and madhouses. I discovered to my delight that an old friend had become judge of the juvenile and domestic-relations court of a large southern city, and I spent hours on his right hand watching human wreckage drift by on a nauseous stream.

And then just about the time that the arteriosclerotic old man of the national tribes decided to sacrifice several million youths to make the world safer for the vested interests, it came to me with a shock that human society, as described by the classical sociologists, was a Platonic idea, a conceptual idealization, having about as much correspondence to the fire and sparkle, the dirt and tears and blood of real life, as Kant's *Ding an sich* has to a pregnant skunk. Nothing in a prosaic army career tended to refute that belated conclusion.

Therefore, when the world had been made secure for the bootleggers, I began to look about for a new set of sociological problems. The old ones I had sweated and grunted over as a student seemed like so much junk. To teach formulae, based for the most part on pure deduction and applicable only in an intellectual fourth dimension, to unspoiled men on the threshold of life, was a form of intellectual dishonesty which I found peculiarly distasteful. I finally decided that the only educational objective worth striving for was to help the student, if I could, better to understand himself and the actual social world in which he lived. But how teach what one knows very little about? How solve problems which have hardly been stated and for the solution of which data are lacking? Such baffling questions brought me to the conclusion that education should be a looking forward rather than a looking backward, and that the function of the teacher is to inspire exploration and discovery rather than to train the memory.

I hope you get the point. We are trying in this course, not to deal with the problems that can be analyzed with the precision and finality of geometrical theorems, for these, it seems to me, are the trivial problems. We are trying to get at the problems that are worth solving. You would find it easy to master Morgan's theory of the evolution of the family and give it back to me verbatim on the final examination. But to think straight about the family as an observable reality shaping personality—that's different. You cannot memorize the latter; you must think about it.

THE FIRE OF FORTITUDE

In the ridiculously short time available for a survey course of this sort, I have tried to achieve two equally important purposes: I have tried to present a provisional thought-model of the broad field of evolutionary sociology, and I have sought to convince you of the value of the scientific habit of mind in dealing with human affairs. It has not been my aim to pour into your brains through the auditory funnel all that has been labeled descriptive and historical sociology. Much has been omitted through malice aforethought. Some important problems have been left to the mercy of your undirected passion for wisdom; some, to the pedagogy of instructors far wiser than I. If I have been able to give you a small guidebook to the elements and first principles of the science of society—a guidebook which you can annotate and supplement as you travel—if I have been able to forewarn you of the muddy places on the narrow path of straight thinking, then perhaps my efforts will not pass unrecorded by the academic Gabriel.

We prefaced this elementary study of human society in the making by a brief consideration of some of the things which sociology is not, and decided that, what-

ever sociology had been or might become, for our purposes, it could be defined as an effort to answer scientifically four questions which some of us think are
worth answering. In this first semester we have addressed ourselves solely to the attempt to answer one
of these questions: How has human society come to be
as it now is? Whether the provisional answer arrived at
is worth the time and energy expended is for you to
decide.

"Good" and "bad" are words tabooed in the kingdom
of science, but in closing permit me for a moment to
deviate into what may seem to be the high moral tone.
We are accustomed, most of us, to look upon society
and human affairs through the stained windows of
emotion and prejudice. Science, like an austere and
overscrupulous old-maid, holds up a skinny finger and
says in a cracked voice: "Stop, listen more attentively,
look more carefully with these." And she hands us
microscopes, and vibration recorders, and statistical
methods. But even at the risk of being misinterpreted,
I would emphasize, here at the end of the dusty road
we've been traveling, that science has no instruments of
investigation that can be used outside the narrow realm
of sensory impression. No one believes more firmly
than I do in the power of science to transform human
life; and no one clings more tenaciously to the faith

that east of the rising sun and west of the evening star lie flowered fields in which our fancy still may play. There are other moods of the human spirit than the scientific, and not all the ponderous formulae of bio-metrika can cramp their enthusiasms. The mysteries of birth and death transcend the chemical equation. There are dreams of the sleeping and the waking mind that make silly the reaction tests of psychologists. Love is more—much more—than all the chromosomes and all the gonads can tell us. The sadness that dwells in the heart of beauty becomes articulate only in the bitter sweetness of a Chopin nocturne. And I have never seen the microscope that could fathom the unclouded life-dawn in the eyes of children, or the sage who could explain the alchemy whereby every beat of a certain heart becomes of more import to a man than the ruin of a universe. Science has not, as I have doubtless said before, robbed life of its mystery nor us of our faith in life's possibilities. It has limited its field, rigidly defined its terms, definitely stated its postulates, arbitrarily se-lected its standards of truth. Further than this it does not seek to go.

But science has also its romance and its dreams, and there are scientists—good ones, I am told—whose "senti-mentality never lays it down to slumber without looking under the bed for the possible beloved." The inevitable transitoriness—the daily death of its new-born "truths"

—gives to science the aspect of a great adventure. For these laws and hypotheses which today we enunciate so solemnly tomorrow will become the intellectual toys of those who lag behind in the slow march of the human mind. Science seeks an ever receding goal, and the scientist realizes that his only contribution is, as Havelock Ellis has suggested, in enlightening for a little while the darkness of the path that others after him will tread. We can, therefore, you see, be scientists and still be believers in the efficacy of Aladdin's wonderful lamp. But we must be one at a time—that is the main point.

In a world wherein nothing is predictable save death and the radio broadcasting of "Holy Night" at Christmas time, the conclusion seems inescapable that only the experimental attitude is permissible for enlightened minds. Is there, in addition, any moral to adorn this tale we've been telling about the making of human society? Are there any implications for our personal philosophies of life? I should like to present a few inductions from this fantastic business of culture-building. Let us reëxamine hurriedly the social world in which we live and move and the factors which have made it. We can then perhaps guess more accurately what it all means for us as individuals, each with his own peculiar traits and his own peculiar aspirations.

We of the Western World live today in a remarkable period of transition, from what we all know to what is known to none save God. We live in the twilight of old idols, in what Nietzsche called the *Götterdämmerung*. The ancient faiths and the eternal verities—in religion, in ethics, in philosophy, even in science—are crumbling into dust. In the gathering darkness of this latest *ancien régime* we watch, with something of disdain and little of regret, the once rigid and unbendable boundary lines of intellectual and ethical areas melt and blend and reshape themselves in unwonted forms that thrill rather than frighten us by their novelty. The puny protests of the elders are beaten down by the horse-laughs and the raucous credos of a new generation, a generation that knows not reverence, that does not bow and scrape to the royal robes of divine or of secular authority.

It is an age of contrasts. Vast material wealth, rainbow-hued and lustrous, jostles elbows with the gray rags of a poverty so filthy and degrading that sensitive souls cannot contemplate it without physical or spiritual nausea. Puritanism suppresses the best literature and outlaws perfidious alcohol, while the crime rate rises and the birth rate falls and the younger set goes to the devil in its own sweet way. Einstein revises Newton; Freud, Jung, and Adler explore the *terra incognita* of repressed desires; Watson annihilates the instinct-hypothesis, and Millikan dissects the atom; while almost at the same time Lodge, Doyle, and Coué resurrect

[33]

animism, witchcraft, and voodooism, and the fundamentalists refute the doctrine of evolution by an appeal to Holy Writ. A thousand iconoclasts are blasting at the Rock of Ages, yet the established church, serene and unabashed, continues to excommunicate its clergy who question the Virgin Birth. Americanism, now in the guise of Luskism, now in the shroud-like habiliments of the Ku Klux Klan, now in the Service false faces of Rotary and Kiwanis, girds up its loins against the enemies of the Constitution, only to find itself arrayed against a million loyal citizens who doubt whether the Constitution is worth defending. The tide of democracy rises, leveling a thousand political, legal, and social inequalities, until the Defenders of the People's Rights cry "There are no inequalities" and predict that within a decade every parliament in Europe will be controlled by Labor. Opposed to this offensive egalitarianism stand the valiant Canutes of experimental psychology and defensive biology, sweeping back the waves of democracy with their intelligence tests and Nordic myths, telling us that we must substitute for the aristocracy of wealth and special privilege the recently discovered aristocracy of brains. It is an age of amazing and disconcerting contrasts.

It is an age of revolt. The bovine acquiescence in preordained social institutions that was the mark of the age of innocence is thrown into the discard of dramatic and literary caricature. Into life's Holy of Holies rush the roughshod radicals, stirred to frenzy by the fanfares of notoriety. They challenge the authority, the power, and the desirability of sanctioned marriage, of the family, of the community, of the state, of the church, and of Almighty God. They match the recessional with hymns of hate; and what we used to call the good old ways, they now name exploitation, something wherewith to keep congealed the Promethean fire that burns in the hearts of the boobery.

To those who watch this darkling plain from afar off, who find, perhaps in neurotic inadequacy, the power to stand philosophically aloof, who sometimes discern a ludicrous and vulgar disproportion between the excitement and its cause, who believe that flies buzz most loudly over dungheaps, there constantly recurs the provocative question, "Why?" Man alone of all God's creatures asks that question Why? and, in asking it, signs perhaps the death warrant of his own happiness. Or—who knows?—he may thereby perchance acquire that dexterity in intellectual gymnastics which is for many men the sole consolation of the lonesome latter years, and—shall I say?—the only *raison d'être* of the higher education.

Why the chaos and the contrasts, the clamor and the iconoclasm? This course, however pretentious its spacious architecture, has not been an attempt to give the final answer to this alliterative Why—the Why of contemporary civilization. But it has been an effort to indicate where the answer must be sought if it is ever to be found. Let me indulge for a little while in the luxury of a hasty résumé.

A billion years ago the Ironic Artificer brought together in magic combination those tiny electronic universes which now go by the names of carbon, hydrogen, oxygen, nitrogen, sulphur, and phosphorus. Three lusty cheers resounded in Heaven as the first protozoan timidly tried out his dimpled pseudopodia in the scorching archaeozoic slime. Ages upon ages of agonizing evolution passed, and then one hot Thursday afternoon the grandfather of old *Pithecanthropus erectus* climbed down from his arboreal boudoir and stood up on his hind legs. Here was the first faint intimation of the Babbitt that was to be. It required another million years of cortical development before our grisly ancestors could discern the advantage of chipping flint; but once they started that monkey business they were monkeys no longer. With the first hatchet man leaped to another evolutionary plane. At first with a snail-like pace, then with ever increasing velocity, over a vast period of three hundred thousand years, material culture piled up and diversified. The collective struggle of *Homo sapiens* for survival and advantage, beginning in a sort of magico-religious blur, developed with incredible slowness into the complicated institutional arrangements of contemporary society, into behavior nexuses in which sense and nonsense, beauty and ugliness, tolerance and intolerance, are inextricably interlaced. However fantastic and irrational any particular culture pattern may appear, we know that its form and content do not and cannot transcend the limits set by the biological nature of man and by the nature of this planet on which man is doomed for a brief span to chase the will-o'-the-wisps of his funny dreams.

Thus each of us is born into a culturized world already gray and somber with age. We arrive in about the same condition, biologically, as Cro-Magnon babies used to arrive. The cultural crazy quilt of our particular group wraps itself about us from the moment of birth, and the heritage of the past is engrafted into our plastic neurones by the omnipresent family. We bawl and puke and scratch our way through the darkness of infancy, childhood, and adolescence to the semblance of individuality. We become socialized, most of us, but biographical selection saves us usually from being just rubber stamps. Socialized, we get into crowds and act accordingly. We learn to coöperate and we learn to fight and, in learning, come to realize that it is almost impossible to get along with other people and quite impossible to get along without them. It takes us twenty-five years to put aside childish things; by fifty we have acquired a little sense;

then, just when we begin to understand what it's all about, we die. A few rare spirits, realizing that life has no meaning save the meaning one gives it, no value save the value one puts upon it, decide that it isn't life that matters but the courage and the laughter one brings to it. These are the aristocrats.

In the developmental process whereby culture has come to be as it now is, and in the developmental process whereby personalities emerge from particular cultural settings, are to be found all the whys and wherefores of contemporary civilization. Our ignorance of these processes is still appalling, but the only motto befitting aristocrats is that of Ulysses: "To strive, to seek, to find, and not to yield." Not to yield even when we realize, as those must who look with seeing eyes upon a cosmic ferment purposeless and unmoral, that the magnitude of the trivial is the key to the riddle of man's life. For we start, you perceive, with the accident of birth, follow a zigzagged path, pushed now here, now there, by scraps of paper, bits of string, the incense of summer flowers, a girl's face glimpsed in a crowd, the ardent glory of April moonlight, the ebony of fear, and the scarlet shadow of rage, until we reach the inevitable mischance of death. But in this groping and fumbling some of us, fortunately, come upon that ineluctable truth long ago discovered by a sage whose name and whose words I have forgotten but whose thought was

[38]

essentially this: that it is easy to live in the world according to the world's ways, and in solitude according to one's own; but the difficult part is to keep, in the traffic of the world, the independence of solitude. Very difficult, I assure you, but that way alone lies sanity and poise and the peace that passeth the understanding of morons, however eminent.

And so, in spite of doubts, fears, and statistics, faith and hope survive. In a world wherein all things seem to shift and change and then utterly to fade away, as twilight shadows on an ancient tapestry, there abideth always beauty, laughter, love—these three, the Blessed Trinity of aristocratic and pagan minds. And whatever may be the effect upon the final examination, and however dangerously close it may come to sentimentality, I make this my valedictory: that it matters little whether you retain in memory the facts and theories with which we have perhaps merely bemused ourselves these many weary months; it matters only that through worship of the aforementioned Blessed Trinity you keep burning always at white heat the living fire of fortitude. For when that goes out, the rest is madness—just plain, stark madness, in the darkness of which there is no beauty and no laughter and no love.

YOUTH AND THE MORAL CODE

I think it was a character in one of Dickens' novels who, when called upon to write an essay on Chinese Metaphysics, turned to the encyclopedia, read first the article on China, then the article on Metaphysics, put the two together, and called the product Chinese Metaphysics. Perhaps you will say that I am following the same grotesque methodology when I contend that any worth-while discussion of the relation of youth to the moral code should be prefaced by a statement of what we mean by youth and what we mean by the moral code. I shall at least, however, avoid some of the anticipated criticism by turning not to the encyclopedia but to my own unconscious plagiarisms during the past few years. What, then, in the first place is youth?

Those who have a Pythagorean faith in the explanatory adequacy of numbers and a becoming reverence for Biblical physiology, will not hesitate to answer that since the vouchsafed life of man is three-score years and ten, youth is the period from birth to the end of adolescence, the golden span wherein we gather the rosebuds until the gaunt shadow of Thirty falls athwart the path, to mark the end of dreaming. But those of us who know the mendacity of figures and distrust all statistics, even those of Jehovah, are not satisfied with the usual chronologies. The oldest person I know is a girl of eighteen who is incapable of responding to any important stimulus unless her cortical neurones are vigorously titillated by the fumes of synthetic gin. And the youngest person I ever met was a grandmother of sixty Aprils who expected, and found, around each corner of the Main Street of life a new and glorious adventure. Herein, it seems to me, lies the first desiderated distinction. Youth cannot be proved by genealogical tables, nor can the heart of youth be measured by the crazy yardsticks of mathematics. There is youth chronological and youth psychological. Not only mercy, but youthfulness, comes for many with the first gray hair; and there is more than literary affectation in the statement that some people must grow old to enter the kingdom of youth. Yet God moves in mysterious ways, and in a world where human striving is grievously impeded by the sluggishness of aging glands, it comes about that physical youth and mental youth for the most part coincide. Thus do all things work together for the greater glory of Jehovah and the further corroboration of Scriptural pronouncements.

It remains forever true, however, that youth is, above all things, an attitude of mind. I would avoid, if possible, the mysticism consequent upon using carelessly the jargon of psychology, and I therefore hasten to add that by attitude of mind I mean nothing more than a consolidation of emotion, instinct, and habit which gives to those truly youthful a tendency to react to their life conditions in certain observable ways. Youth, thus understood, has its own distinguishable attributes, and it may be not unprofitable to enumerate and briefly comment upon some of them.

Youth is naïve. It faces the pompous nonsense of the social heritage with an engaging simplicity, and confounds the elders with an innocent "What of it?" With unconscious ingenuousness it forgets what should be remembered and remembers what should be forgotten. Eddie Foy, coperpetrator of the Seven Little Foys, used to tell a story that is somewhat apropos. One of his friends had a little girl by the name of Marion. On her eleventh birthday Marion was being bedecked in finery by her mother for the party which was to mark the glorious event. "Now, Marion," said her mother, putting on the finishing touches, "if at the party any older person should ask you your name, you must say, 'Marion, sir.' And if he should ask your age, you must say, 'Eleven years, sir.' And if he should ask, 'Who made you?' you must say, 'God made me, sir.' Thus prepared, Marion tripped off to the festivities. Surely enough a kindly old gentleman approached her shortly

after her arrival and solemnly went through the anticipated catechism: 'And what is your name, little girl?'
'Marion, sir.' 'And how old are you, Marion?' 'Eleven
years, sir.' 'And who made you, Marion?' At that
Marion paused and scratched her head. Finally she
answered, 'Mother did tell me the man's name, sir, but
I've forgotten it.' "

Youth is plastic. Age refers each person, each thing,
each new situation to a conceptual pigeonhole and
smirks complacently at its irrefutable explanations. But
youth laughs at rigid categories, finds its Q.E.D.'s in
the autonomic functions, and when the universe is in-
compatible with its philosophy, changes not the universe,
after the manner of the elders, but the philosophy. From
which it follows both that youth is skeptical and that
youth is esthetic. It is skeptical on the emotional rather
than on the intellectual level; and it affirms always that
it matters little whether a thing be true or good or
useful, it matters only that it be beautiful. Youth faces
frankly the wretchedness of God's handiwork and seeks
salvation by refashioning an ugly world in the likeness
of its dreams.

Youth is rebellious. This, I think, is its most per-
vasive characteristic, for in a sense it is the inevitable
corollary of each of the other attributes. To acquiesce
may be, as Mr. Cabell has suggested, the great lesson.
But the Demiurge makes youth find in submission the

[43]

unpardonable sin against the Holy Ghost of life, and in authority only a *casus belli*. When revolt ceases, there is the beginning of age. Against what youth eternally rebels and about the real nature of that freedom for which it clamors so insistently, we shall have occasion to inquire later.

Naïveté, plasticity, skepticism, estheticism, and rebelliousness—these, it seems to me, are the outstanding traits of the youthful attitude of mind. And no matter what one's age, nevertheless if one has these mental traits he is still young. So much for youth. What of the moral code?

The time has happily passed when one needs to preface a discussion of morality with quotations either from the Biblical prophets or the ethical philosophers. From the Stoics of ancient Greece to contemporary Fundamentalists, philosophers and theologians endeavored to find the meaning of good and evil in divine revelation, by prolonged introspection, or in ruminating the nasty social habits of barbarians. What they found was often interesting, is now deemed essential in college curricula, but had the disadvantage, for scientific purposes, of being almost invariably contrary to fact.

Under the brilliant leadership of Spencer, Bagehot, Westermarck, Sumner, and Hobhouse, sociologists set forth to discover the meaning of morality in a dispassionate study of human behavior. They started with the

general assumption that if one wants to know how
human beings behave and why they behave that way
the best method of finding out is, not to dissect the human organism, not to watch responses to stimuli in a psychological laboratory, not even to read the Socratic *Discourses* or the *Republic* of Plato, but to observe, measure,
and classify, without bias or preconviction, the folkways
which arise in response to actual life conditions. In the
analysis of folkways, they held, will be found all that
the scientific student of human society needs to know
about morals. While the pioneers often used methods of
investigation which have since become obsolete, while
many of the facts from which they generalized have
been discarded, while they were often guilty of allowing
their personal preferences to push them into absurd
fallacies, their basic assumption remains today the point
of departure for sociological analyses of the moral life
of mankind. For certainly if we are ever to know "why
we behave like human beings," we must first know how
human beings behave; and that knowledge is not de-
ducible from the mysteries of the endocrine glands,
descriptions of reflex arcs, the principles of heredity, or
the philosophy of Immanuel Kant. The folkways *are*
how human beings behave.

It is a matter of common knowledge that sociologists
and ethnologists in their quest for the meaning of morality and its conditioning factors found in their peregri-

YOUTH AND THE MORAL CODE

nations through time and space an amazing diversity of opinion and practice. In Western civilization the deliberate and premeditated murder of the aged by their near relatives would be regarded as a most heinous crime; but among the Chuckchee such murder has been interpreted as the performance of a sacred obligation. To speak, in this country, to one's mother-in-law may perhaps be followed by unexpected and sometimes serious consequences; but among the Yahi of California it would have been immoral. For a hundred per cent American who offered his wife as a bedmate to a guest, no punishment could be too severe; but the refusal of a Masai to do just that would, by the standards of his country, be equally reprehensible. That a hitherto unmarried bride should be a virgin is not debatable in this part of the world; but a Toda girl who had not been deflowered before puberty is abused and reproached and Toda men may refuse to marry her. Among the ancient Jews a man was morally bound to marry the widow of his deceased brother; until quite recently an Englishman who did that was regarded as incestuous. In Japan young people in love whose parents have forbidden them to marry frequently commit suicide, and their filial piety is generally applauded; among us suicide following parental disapproval would probably bring down upon the parents the wrath of an outraged community. Illustrations are legion; fat volumes may be found in

[46]

the libraries filled with examples of this bewildering moral diversity. To most educated people the facts have become commonplaces; to those trained to regard the moral code as something handed by Yahveh to Moses on tablets of stone, the sociological survey is disconcerting. Indeed if one sticks fairly closely to the assembled data, the conclusion seems inescapable that morality is simply conformity to a social norm and that there are as many social norms as there are culture areas on the face of the earth. There is nothing, one may assert without wandering far from the truth, by our standards so brutal, indecent, and degrading—murder, rape, theft, incest, cannibalism, slavery—that it has not at some time and place been socially approved. In the light merely of the unclassified and unanalyzed data, intuitionalism is seen to be a philosophic monstrosity, and the "still, small voice" appears not to emanate from the heavenly broadcasting station but to be, as Professor James Harvey Robinson once suggested, "the still, small voice of the herd."

But the problem is far from being solved by this initial conclusion. A myriad of questions immediately arise to plague the investigator. Why does the herd speak at all? What sort of behavior, if any, elicits neither approval nor condemnation? Why does the voice of the human herd enunciate so many different thou-shalt's and thou-shalt-not's at various times and places? Are there no modes of conduct to which it universally says Yes or No? Why do individuals pay heed to the voice of the herd, and to what extent do they? How does the moral code of a social group come to be as it is? With what observable and measurable circumstances and conditions, biological, geographic, cultural, psychological, are moral variations through time and space correlated? How is each new generation fitted to the moral scheme into which it is thrust by the accident of birth? What is the relation of religion to morals, of law to morals, of ethics to morals?

Despite the appalling vastness of the "literature of the subject," it would be ridiculous bravado to pretend that sociology can give the final scientific answer to all, or indeed to any, of these questions. In the first place, moral, and immoral, practices elude, thank God, the scrutiny not only of the scientist but of the uplifter, and the professed moral code, in civilized and in preliterate societies, is never an accurate reflection of how human beings behave. Criminal statistics in advanced cultures are notoriously unreliable; for the simpler peoples they are unavailable. The questionnaire method is in well-merited disrepute. Even "expert" opinion has no factual basis. If a hypothetical ethnologist from Melanesia should ask a person of Mayflower ancestry whether premarital unchastity and abduction are immoral in America, he would undoubtedly receive a lusty affirmative, reinforced by statutory citations regarding fornication. Only a postgraduate Fundamentalist would accept this as a precise description of extra-connubial intimacies in the United States. On the other hand, contrary to much ethnological dogmatism, the disparity, in primitive societies, between traditional morals and actual life is far greater than the pious pronouncements of the old men of the tribes would lead the superficial investigator to suspect. Even breaches of the exogamous rules are not infrequent. According to Malinowski, to the native libertine in the Trobriand Archipelago the breach of exogamy is indeed a "specially interesting and spicy form of erotic experience." There are, in short, no instruments of investigation whereby the scientific sociologist can measure conformity to or deviation from traditional moral codes, or compare degrees of obedience to law and custom either in civilized or in preliterate societies.

But neither by the paucity of existing data nor by the inadequacy of current research methods is the sociologist constrained to abandon the study of morals. Though he realizes that, in the present stage of knowledge, his conclusions must needs be provisional—scientific guesses—he feels nevertheless that a clear statement of the problem is imperative and that what we really do know should be said with clarity and precision. For it is one of the many sad but interesting commentaries upon human nature that men pretend to the greatest knowledge and are guilty of the most offensive dogmatism about those very problems which are least amenable to analysis and understanding. On all sides today one hears interminable chatter about moral codes and moral practices and moral laws; and most of the self-appointed pundits are obviously afflicted with that pernicious logorrhea which bespeaks the vacuous mind. If sociology merely indicates the limits of our knowledge, or, to put it otherwise, the extent of our ignorance; if it does nothing more than erect a few scientific barriers against the devastating sweep of nonsense masquerading as religious authority or as academic erudition, its efforts will not have been in vain.

In contemplating moral diversity the devout in desperation may ask: Are there no limits to these variations? To that the comparative sociologist replies, Yes; God, in his infinite wisdom and mercy, has set bounds to human caprice. The Eskimo do not prohibit the shooting of partridges, nor do they prescribe ritual bathing in their icy streams; neither do the Melanesians impose taboos upon the walrus. Thus does geography influence the ethical code. The human nervous system seems to be about the same the world over, and in all people there is a point beyond which stimulation brings decreasing returns, a physiological limit to indulgence.

Thus do the biological and psychological forces make for universal righteousness. Moreover, there are limited possibilities in the development of moral codes. If, for example, we classify marriage by the number of parties to the union, we can, mathematics being what it is, get only four varieties: one man to one woman—monogamy; one man to several women—polygamy; one woman to several men—polyandry; several women to several men—sexual communism. All four have been practiced; all four have been socially approved; all four have been socially disapproved. We say monogamy is right—and usually practice polygamy. The Todas say polyandry is right—and usually practice monogamy. Customs differ, codes vary. Good and bad, we perceive, are funny words, and except in graveyards one finds few results that closely resemble their antecedents.

The upshot of sociological investigation seems to be this: that environmental, biological, psychological, and mathematical factors set the limits, very far apart, one must admit, within which develop a vast variety of contradictory and irreconcilable moral codes. Behind each code, constituting its ultimate sanction, are customs, group habits. The specific origins of these customs are lost in mystery; but there are abundant data to warrant the assertion that the customs of any culture group are for the most part unconscious, unreflective, irrational adjustments to the life conditions, either arrived at independently or borrowed, in whole or in part, from other peoples. The moral code, oral or written, is a collection of the taboos and prescriptions, the thou-shalt's and the thou-shalt-not's implicit in the antecedent customs. To the question, Whence this or that particular moral code, the sociologist answers—historical accident. Conscience, hitherto regarded as a God-given device for inculcating the old sturdy virtues of our forefathers, takes on, under the Satanic influence of sociology, a new meaning. "The still, small voice" appears, upon careful research as I said before, to be "the still, small voice of the herd."

From this general point of view and in the light of these well established and widely accepted facts, let us glance for a while, with all due reverence and respect, at the moral doctrine now in vogue in The Land of the Free and the Home of the Brave. We can only speak with certainty, as I previously suggested, of the standards of right and wrong; for in a world where the majority of the species *Homo sapiens* are most of the time encased in brick and mortar, moral practices elude, thank God, the scrutiny of both scientific and religious peep-toms. What do we find in the code? We find the usual savage resentment against the deviate and the nonconformist, the usual unreasoning mandates of the herd. And most conspicuous of all, we find a sex complex, so distinctive, so insistently obtrusive, that it must be regarded as an indispensable part of the American culture pattern. In a brief discussion like this, we may legitimately confine ourselves to American sex morality. Morality in this country, indeed, is usually frankly identified with the intricate body of taboos and prescriptions which controls the sexual relations.

Whence comes this dogma that the most hideous sin is to be detected in illicit sexual practices? The curious American overemphasis upon sex may readily be ascribed, as Professor Harry E. Barnes has pointed out, to business enterprise with its ideal of formal and external purity and to modern Puritanism with its neurotic defense mechanisms. But our sex mores as a whole have a longer history. To trace that history in detail would require several volumes. We should have to begin with the supernaturalistic ethics of our primitive ancestors; we should have to follow the social process whereby the gross sex mores of Jewish tribes were formulated and rationalized in the Ten Commandments and in Just-So stories about Jehovah and Moses; we should have to re-enact the historical tragedies of the triumph of Judaism over Hellenism and of the triumph of Pauline and Augustinian asceticism and sadism over the beneficent tolerance of the teachings of Christ; we should have to show once more how from the strange marriage of Protestantism and capitalism was born the monster of sex bigotry; we should have to resurrect that eminent paranoiac, Immanuel Kant, and demonstrate how he found compensation for his physical frailty and sexual inadequacy in an elaborate philosophical rationalization of the so-called Christian ethic; and finally we should have to explain in an appendix to our story how ages of unreasoning repression have produced that nauseating social psychosis known as Comstockianism. The story has been often told, with amazing skill and convincingness, by the historians of culture. The libraries are open to those who are interested. We are concerned here only with the general conclusions of scientific research. The only acceptable sociological explanation of the current code of sex morality is to be found in the historical process from primitive Judaism to the enlightened evangelism of the late Mr. William Jennings Bryan.

As a result of this historical process and its psychological consequences, we live in a sex-obsessed culture, among purists, vice-crusaders, Babbitts, Rotarians, and Hundred Percenters who are really more engrossed in obscenity and lasciviousness than the worst roués of Paris, Vienna, and Constantinople; in a culture wherein sexual taboos are so multitudinous, so irrational, so positively pernicious that should Socrates return to earth and visit America he would forthwith gulp down the hemlock in sheer disgust. If anyone doubts this absorption in sex, let him glance at the average news stall with its pornographic magazines; let him go to the average show; let him read the columns of the average newspaper; let him listen to the average sermon or even to the average street-corner conversation, or even read this essay. If he doubts the multiplicity of sexual taboos, let him contemplate the laws on marriage, birth control, prostitution, roadside petting, beach costumes, censorship, *ad infinitum.* It may occur to the scientist who makes these observations that the absorption in sex is a function of the sex taboo, or, as the Freudians would say, that every prohibition conceals a desire. Apparently this has never occurred to the uplifters; for they combat lasciviousness by increasing repression, and repression is precisely the cause of the objectionable thing they seek to eliminate. To phrase the whole matter succinctly, and therefore perhaps a little inaccurately, because St. Paul and St. Augustine were sexually abnormal, it is indecent in America today to affirm that sex is a fact.

And now after much meandering we arrive at what you will doubtless consider the main point. "What happens when youth confronts the current moral code?" Opinions differ. We live, I am told, in the twilight of old idols. Ancient faiths and long-cherished dogmas have, from what I can understand, been crumbled by the vandal hands of youth. The feeble protests of the old order which passes are lost in the stalwart clamor of a new world that knows not reverence nor makes obeisance to the mandates of the past. So I have been told. But, frankly, I don't believe it. When I have gone hopefully in quest of this alleged immorality of youth, I have found only the shadow, not the substance of evil. I have found cigarette-smoking, gin-drinking, grotesque muscular coördinations in dancing, vulgar conversation, feeble pretenses of atheism, but of real wickedness I must report a deplorable dearth. Compared to the daily routine of the young person in Renaissance Italy, the wildest parties of our sweet young things are like the innocuous pranks of naughty children. For the devil's advocates, things, I regret to say, look rather dark. The flesh seems willing, but the spirit is weak. Is there anything more pathetic than the loud-mouthed striving of the flapper to be bad, or than the futile little gestures of the radical young man who can't go wrong, no matter how hard he tries? Herein lies the tragedy, that youth with its freshness, its plasticity, its trenchant skepticism, its ennobling estheticism, its Promethean rebelliousness, should be forever wasted. For no matter how bravely youth sets forth, it seems always to return so quickly, mumbling the words of Florian, "To submit is the great lesson." Everywhere I find the sense of guilt, everywhere the restlessness of those whose normal impulses are thwarted by abnormal restraints. I fear that youth, despite its vociferous protests, has not slain the

Dragon. I fear that youth is still in the vise-like grip of the dead hand of the past.

The usual literary and dramatic picture of the immorality of youth does not correspond to the facts as I have found them. It has been distorted, I think, in two ways. It has been distorted, first, by the prodigious verbalization which in American society follows every infraction of a sex taboo. When a girl goes wrong, the fact could adequately be expressed as a digit in a statistical table; it is actually expressed however in column after column in the newspapers, in interminable drool in the magazines, in a novel, or in a play written around the meager situation. We react not to the simple fact that a girl found opportunity to gratify a natural impulse, but to all that a thousand second-rate people think they think about it. The picture of the alleged immorality of youth is further distorted by the activities of the ever-increasing number of Mrs. Grundys, of both sexes, who pollute the stream of contemporary thought. These neurotics are the victims of a psychic conflict between vicious impulses and a morbid ideal of sexual purity. Unable to face their own lasciviousness they project it, by a well-known mental mechanism, into others, and accuse the youth of the land, who unfortunately are quite innocent, of not only wishing but of attaining the delights which they themselves most ardently, though unconsciously, desire. Flaming youth, upon close scrutiny, thus turns out to be a feeble little spark ridiculously magnified by reflection through prurient minds. The analysis is unpleasant and I am loath to continue it. The point I wish to make is that if there is cause for lamentation, it is not that youth has abandoned the moral code but that, in spite of much sound and fury, it still clings to it so tenaciously.

It is lamentable because the disastrous results of the imbecility of the current sex code are everywhere apparent. It renders impossible intelligent sex education, and the ultimate consequences are sexual perversion, insanity, suicide, and marital tragedy. It opposes venereal prophylaxis, and the ravages of syphilis and paresis continue almost unabated. It hinders eugenics and sterilization, and the epileptics and the feeble-minded produce their kind without restraint. It permits barbarous divorce laws, based upon an outworn religious imperative, and the sequel is degraded homes and the geometric increase of human misery. It prohibits birth control, and thereby sentences thousands of women to death or to chronic invalidism, to say nothing of the vast increase in population which makes for lowered standards of living and ultimate disaster. The list is endless and you are doubtless as familiar with it as I am. It is lamentable that youth clings to this code, not only because of these social consequences, but because if change ever comes it must be initiated under the leadership of youth. The old are beyond redemption. Their reflexes have been too rigidly conditioned.

The current moral code in America, especially as it relates to sex, is a survival of primitive supernaturalism and apostolic bigotry. It is perpetuated by the stupidity of parents, and rigidly maintained by Puritan neurotics who are tormented, as Mr. Mencken phrases it, by "the haunting fear that someone, somewhere, may be happy." It was conceived in the hatred of the Elders for that youthful charm and beauty which they had irrevocably lost, and dedicated to the proposition that the sexual impulse is not only sinful but that, officially, it does not exist at all. Against the stone wall of our present moral code youth is broken and wasted. So long as it endures we shall have bitterness and restlessness and revolt. For the moral code in America seeks to thwart and to destroy the strongest human impulse, to degrade below the level of swine the love-life of man. With this code youth can have no compromise. Not until this code is eliminated from human living can we hope for the renaissance of the blessed Hellenic trinity—beauty, laughter, and love. It is for this that youth struggles to free itself from the tentacles of current taboos.

THE PROBLEM OF SOCIAL CONTROL

The promiscuous use of verbal symbols to which several distinct meanings may be attached is especially characteristic of theological disputation, the conversation of flappers, and the literature of sociological theory. That the Lord's anointed and the sweet young things are justified in thus concealing their mental sterility, we will not attempt to refute; that such rhetorical jugglery is, for the scientist, an unpardonable sin, it is doubtless unnecessary to prove. For science, when it becomes articulate, seeks to translate into words the impressions made by the phenomena of the objective world upon the human senses, to describe the various sequences and juxtapositions in laws and generalizations. It is a truism to say that the validity of these generalizations depends upon the degree to which the terms employed can be consistently reapplied to the particular phenomena they are supposed to describe.

It was unfortunate that sociology, already denounced as a mere parasitic growth subsisting upon the outworn truths of moral and social philosophies, should have exposed itself to further criticism by adopting a chaotic terminology. And yet, in the nature of things, this was perhaps inevitable. Each sociologist, limited in his thought by the environment in which he happened to be born and coloring with the pigments of his prejudices the impressions made upon him by that environment, arbitrarily selected phrases with which to describe the social forms and processes under his observation. The sum total of these phrases constitutes the nomenclature of sociology—and the source of untold mental misery for the spiritual stepsons of the pioneers in "the newest science." The confusion arises both because sociologists have used different terms to describe the same things, and because they have used the same terms to describe different things. In the face of such a situation those of us who are afflicted with a fair degree of intellectual honesty and cursed with a predilection for the statistical method are likely to be somewhat dismayed. The problems of social organization, social mind, social control, become analogous to those mathematical problems in which there are one equation, three quantities, and two variables. If we can, however, find the limits of the variables, or establish arbitrary limits, our efforts will not have been wholly in vain. In the hope of attaining such ends we may approach the problem of social control.

The proper answer to the question "What is meant by social control?" is "Which 'social control' do you mean?" There is control that restrains and control that directs.

[61]

THE PROBLEM OF SOCIAL CONTROL

Assuming either one of these meanings, there is control that affects society and control which society effects. There may be control of human conduct and control of the factors by which that conduct is conditioned. And so on, *ad infinitum et ad nauseam*. Enough has been said to warrant the statement that the problem of social control resolves itself into at least three questions: (1) What are the phenomena which the term "social control" has been used to describe or which, identical with or definitely related to the phenomena so described, have actually been otherwise described? (2) Can the term "social control" be applied with scientific precision to any or all of these phenomena? (3) If not, are there phenomena of which the term "social control" is descriptive and which can be described by that term without confusion or ambiguity? We will attempt to answer these questions in the order in which they are stated, beginning with an analysis of the Spencerian theory of social control.

A society, according to Spencer, is something more than a mere aggregate of human beings. Besides juxtaposition there must be coöperation. But concerted actions, to be lasting and effective, must be organized. There must be agencies by which the actions are adjusted in their "times, amounts, and kinds," and in order that there may be different kinds of actions there must be division of labor among the coöperators. The

[62]

THE PROBLEM OF SOCIAL CONTROL

totality of the relatively persistent forms of organized coöperative activity constitutes the social organization. The various forms of organized coöperative activity, Spencer calls "institutions." The structural and functional phenomena of institutions is the subject matter of sociology. Inasmuch as Spencer uses the term control to mean the regulation of human conduct, and inasmuch as all institutions regulate human conduct, the Science of Sociology would become the Science of Social Control. But Spencer designates as controlling agencies those institutions which constantly carry on directive and restraining functions only. Hence, the regulation of human conduct by means of ceremonial, political, and ecclesiastical institutions is social control, in the Spencerian sense.

The origin and evolution of these controlling institutions are treated at great length in the three volumes of the *Principles of Sociology*. We are told therein that the earliest and most general form of control is ceremony which originates in fear. The primitive man fears those living persons who are stronger than himself, and he fears the ghosts of the dead who have become in his mind causal agents for everything unfamiliar. In the effort to propitiate these personal powers, seen and unseen, he modifies his conduct into behavior expressing affection or behavior expressing subjection. Before the chieftain whose prowess is made manifest by the tro-

[63]

phies he has gathered, the primitive man bows low his head, just as we today go through certain conventional antics in the presence of the man whose floors are carpeted with the skins of tigers shot in South Africa. To the powerful and efficient man the savage voluntarily surrenders parts of his body. Such mutilation expresses submission and because of this becomes a propitiatory ceremony—a ceremony which survives today in the tatooings of sailors and the cropped heads of the inmates of Sing Sing. From the ceremony of mutilation develops the custom of present-giving, the modern forms of which are taxation, the Sunday collection plate, the exchange of neckties and handkerchiefs at Christmas, and perhaps the veil of flowers which covers the fresh grave. And so on through the long list of ceremonies: visits, obeisances, forms of address, titles, badges and costumes. The indefinite control effected by these observances, at first unorganized, soon acquires a definite organization. The direction of the propitiatory rites expressing subordination to the living and the dead becomes the function of certain officials, forerunners of the toreadors of spirituality who occupy our modern pulpits and the majestic personalities who preside in our police courts. This ceremonial organization, evolving from indefinite simplicity to definite complexity, ultimately dwindles and passes into mere civility and politeness, "as the struc-

THE PROBLEM OF SOCIAL CONTROL

tures, political and ecclesiastical, which exercise controls more definite and detailed, usurp its functions."

As the relationships between conqueror and conquered become fixed, as headship, originally transitory, becomes permanent through the "transmission of position and property to the eldest son of the eldest continually," political organization differentiates from ceremonial observance. Individual wills, at first constrained by the joint wills of the group, are now more definitely constrained by the will of a regulative agency which the group evolves. The structure of this regulative agency is always a triune structure. There is a chief or leader; there is a superior minority among whom the chief is, at first, merely the most conspicuous; there is an inferior majority who modify by expressions of approval and dissent the actions of the chief and the group of leading men. Out of this triune structure, the general form of which is always retained, have evolved all political and ecclesiastical organizations, past and present.

From those ceremonial observances which consist of propitiatory rites directed towards the ghosts of departed kings and chiefs, there develop the multiform ecclesiastical institutions. At first not clearly distinguishable from political institutions, they gradually differentiate into independent organizations performing functions quite different from those exercised by the state. Without carrying further the analysis of Spencer's theory of social control, except to say that as society passes from militancy to industrialism control is effected more by voluntary than compulsory coöperation, we may summarize that theory in a definition: *Social Control is the modification of human conduct into "behavior" expressing affection or "behavior" expressing subjection by means of ceremonial, political, and ecclesiastical institutions.*

With the contention of Spencer that the earliest form of control originates in the fear of some superior power, Professor Giddings does not entirely agree. Neither does he accept as a complete explanation the utilitarian theories of Hobbes, Locke, and Rousseau. On the contrary, he asserts that control may and does originate in other ways than through the definite perception of an ultimate utility or the fear of the living and the dead. In any group of individuals subjected to common stimulation there is a differential reaction. Some men react promptly and effectively, others slowly and awkwardly. To the leadership of the promptly and effectively reacting minority, the less fortunate members of the group voluntarily, almost instinctively, submit themselves. This unenforced subordination is not necessarily the result of fear, nor is it, consciously, a means for attaining certain previsualized ends. Rather may it be described as the result of a vague feeling on the part of the less effectively reacting members of the group that they can best extricate themselves from an unpleasant or dangerous situation by following blindly the lead of those individuals who manifest the ability to solve the problem by which the whole group is confronted. "A more vigorous common reaction and a livelier consciousness of kind" convert these "dynamic" men—in the parlance of everyday life, these "born leaders"—into a ruling group. Because there is always a differential reaction to common stimulation, there is in every group a power, personal or social, that either does or can obtain the obedience of practically all members of the community. This power which obtains the obedience of the component units of any social group is sovereignty. The "requisition, direction, and organization" of the obedience thereby obtained is government.

Under various circumstances sovereignty assumes various modes to which correspond various types of government. The prevailing mode of sovereignty is determined by the general mental development of the population. The prevailing type of government is determined by the general social conditions. Where the population is predominantly ideomotor in its reactions, sovereignty is manifested in the power of the strong personality to command obedience. If he exercises this power directly and unconditionally, because of the chaotic and insecure social conditions, the government may be described as an absolute minority rule. If, because

THE PROBLEM OF SOCIAL CONTROL

the community is capable of spontaneous coöperation, he is restricted in the exercise of his power, the government becomes a limited minority rule. When the population is predominantly ideo-emotional in its reactions, sovereignty is manifested in the power of a superior class to inspire obedience. As in the case of personal sovereignty and under like conditions, the government of this minority may be absolute or limited. When revolutionary conditions, political or industrial, obtain in society, absolute majority rule, exercised directly and unconditionally, becomes the form of government, and sovereignty is manifested in the power of a fanatical majority of the dogmatic-emotional population to compel obedience. Lastly, when a community is composed of individuals approximately equal in ability and in condition, the government takes the form of a limited majority rule, and sovereignty becomes the power of the enlightened group to evoke obedience "through a rational appeal to intelligence and conscience."

We have seen that sovereignty, according to Professor Giddings, is a power—a social force—that obtains obedience, and that government is the direction of obedience or the utilization of obedience as a means to certain ends. What are these ends and how are they deter-mined? They are determined, says Professor Giddings, by various policies, internal, external, external-internal. Internal policies have for their object the achievement of certain relations or conditions among the members of a social group. According to whether they are policies of unity, of liberty, of equality, they aim to perfect the solidarity of the group, to permit individuation, to establish an equality of liberty and opportunity. External policies have for their object the achievement of certain relations between one social group and another. They aim to subjugate, to exploit, or to assist. External-internal policies, through militarism, exploitation, or peace, achieve certain relations both among the members of a group and between one group and another.

It is evident that the essence of that kind of control which has been briefly described in the foregoing paragraphs is the obtaining of obedience for the achievement of certain social relationships. That this is not the only kind of control recognized in Professor Giddings' sociological system will be readily anticipated by those even superficially acquainted with that system. There is, more explicitly, a controlling power which arises and functions quite differently from sovereignty and government. To understand the genesis, the development, and the nature of this power, we must approach the problem more definitely from the evolutionary viewpoint.

The struggle of all organisms for adaptation in order to live and perpetuate their kind is the fundamental fact of the universe of living matter. This struggle for adaptation is a struggle for existence, since organisms unadapted to their environment cannot survive. Now organisms which are adjusted to practically identical or to very similar conditions are necessarily alike. In other words, the struggle for existence creates types, or "modal" groupings of similar organisms. Continued like reactions to common stimulation convert modal groups into communities; supplemented by awareness of common reaction, they convert the community into conscious society. The members of this society have a notion of a type or kind, to which they in part conform. They constitute, in fact, a type or norm or mode. They have learned through experience the relation of type-conformity to group efficiency and survival. Therefore they display a "dominant antipathy" to certain variates.

As a means to limiting variation a social constraint is consciously evolved which exerts its influence upon all component units of the group. The unconscious evolutionary process which created modal groups is now supplemented by discipline which the groups create and apply with conscious intent. The common intent or purpose of a group to discipline its members is a product of "innumerable suggestions, examples, imitations, and discussions and of a diffused approval or opposition." It is, in other words, a product of what Professor Giddings calls "primary social pressure." The actual disciplinary achievement through consciously exerted social constraint is secondary social pressure. Statute law is an expression of social intent and is therefore a measure of primary social pressure. The actual effect of these laws upon human conduct is a measure of secondary social pressure. This pressure, primary or secondary, or both, which the group brings to bear upon its component units, is social self-control.

We are thus forced to the conclusion that Professor Giddings has advanced two theories of social control, or rather may it be said that he has theorized about two different kinds of social control. The first can be described as the power, in whatever mode of sovereignty it manifests itself, which obtains the obedience of the component units of a social group and directs and organizes that obedience through the mechanism of some type of government; the second, as a group-pressure acting upon all individuals to limit variation from type.

We must at this point reverse the evolutionary process. Passing from the theories of Spencer and Giddings to the theory of Professor Ross, we move from relatively definite, coherent complexity to relative indefinite, incoherent simplicity, and our contained emotion undergoes a parallel transformation. That this seemingly cynical remark is not made unadvisedly will doubtless be admitted by those familiar with the writings of the gentleman from Wisconsin. Professor Ross's book might not inadequately be described as a money-making medium for the pyrotechnic display of parti-colored rheto-

ric. As a scientific description of social phenomena and
social processes, the work is not incomparable to the
Gospel according to St. John. When we read the dedi-
cation, "To my master—Lester F. Ward," we are pro-
foundly impressed with the deep and abiding truth of
the Shakespearean contention that "the evil which men
do lives after them." Inhibiting, however, a not un-
natural tendency to criticize rather than analyze, let us
see how Professor Ross discourses upon this slippery and
elusive problem of social control.

In the preface to his book on control, the author points
out that Social Psychology, or the science of the "psychic
interplay between man and his environing society," has
two aspects: social ascendancy and individual ascendancy. Social ascendancy is divided into social influence,
or the unintended, purposeless domination of society
over the individual; and social control, or that domination "which is intended and which fulfills a function in
the life of society." Individual ascendancy, embracing
such topics as invention, leadership, the rôle of great
men, is defined as the domination of the individual over
society. Having thus neatly and nicely surveyed the
field of Social Psychology, Professor Ross obligingly in-
forms us that his book will be limited to a treatment
of one subdivision of that field, namely, social ascendancy. Inasmuch as we subsequently come upon chapters
devoted to leadership, personality, and art, we are per-

haps justified in wondering whether Professor Ross was trying to fool us in the preface, whether his careful classification was not just a verbal structure, "full of sound and fury, signifying nothing." But we are lapsing again into the mood critical. Let us proceed.

Assuming that human beings in a state of nature would exhibit towards one another a sonorous and scratchy pugnacity analogous to that which mars the nocturnal processions of back-fence felines, Professor Ross points out that the problem of social control is a problem of ascertaining by what means the natural human struggle is narrowed and limited. Man, not being the "good ape" alleged by a well-known French philosopher, would be forever flying at the throat of his fellow man, were it not for the constraining effect of certain forces and factors.

What are these factors which account for the absence of the expected disharmony? First of all, the moral capital of the individual. We would hardly have expected such a concession to sin-ridden humanity. But so it is stated—"the moral capital of the individual." Its components are sympathy, sociability, sense of justice, and resentment. To what concrete realities these names are supposed to correspond, we do not know. They are inherent qualities. In other words, all men are by nature sympathetic, sociable, just, and resentful. Already we have been told that human beings are naturally antagonistic to one another. Professor Ross's shameless inconsistency is at times offensively feminine. But let us see how the components of man's moral capital are defined.

Sympathy is an instinct, correlated in some inexplicable way with the last stages of puberty and manifesting itself in a regard for the woes of other people. Sociability is the gregarious instinct. The sense of justice is the sense of "fair play" growing out of the consciousness that the feelings of the *alter* are very similar to the feelings of the *ego*. Resentment is a sort of defensive reflex which impels you, when hit, to hit back. After these illuminating explanations we have, of course, no difficulty in understanding that the moral capital of the individual is necessarily the basis for a "natural order" in society.

But this natural order, spontaneously arising, breaks down as society differentiates. There arises the need of social control. Exactly why and how this natural order, based as it is on inherent human attributes, crashes into chaos unless perpetuated by "means of control," doubtless Professor Ross's Greek-like disdain of vulgar reality prevents him explaining. All we can say is that unless harmony were maintained by certain social agencies, humanity would rush pell-mell "back to nature." The social devices which prevent this precipitous reversion are what Professor Ross calls the means of control. They

THE PROBLEM OF SOCIAL CONTROL

are divided into two classes: (A) Means of influencing
the feeling of individuals in ways that shall conduce to
harmony, obedience, and respect for the rights of others;
(B) Means of molding the judgment of individuals to
accomplish the same end. Let us look for a moment
at the exhibits in Class A.

First of all, there is Public Opinion, an integration
of public judgment, public sentiment, public action. Public opinion makes itself effective through sanctions of
opinion, of intercourse, and of violence. Then there is
law, which reinforces public opinion, and belief, which
supplements both by supernatural sanctions. Social suggestion, working through examples and expectation,
manifesting itself in education and custom, plays its part
in modifying the unruliness of the individual; and social religion, or the soul-stirring conviction that there is
a bond of ideal relationships among the members of a
society, orients the feelings of men to the advantage of
social order. Then there is ceremony, or formality in
personal intercourse, which has its roots in servility and
self-respect; there is art—"all those means whereby an
idea wins peculiar force through its form of expression"
—dear old art, arousing the passions, kindling sympathy,
exploiting the aesthetic sense and the sense of the sub-
lime, perfecting social symbols, fascinating with new
types, in short, taming the "blond beast" man into a
sweet domestic animal; and lastly, there is the strong

[75]

magnetic personality to whom voluntary subordination and deference is a primitive social fact. Such are the means which influence the feelings. What are the means which influence the judgment?

First in the list comes enlightenment, enlightenment as to the results of an individual's acts to himself, enlightenment as to the results of an individual's acts to others. Next in order comes illusion, or the imaginative faculty which enables us to believe that it is worth while to play the game of life, and by certain rules, when we could just as logically believe the contrary. Lastly, there are social valuations, evolved by a process of trial and error which results in the selection and survival of some as ethical elements, maintained by tradition.

Following the analysis of the means of control, Professor Ross dilates variously and dreamily upon class control and upon the vicissitudes of social control in general, until he reaches page four hundred and eleven, at which point, discovering that he has by no means exhausted his rich journalistic vocabulary, he decides to talk some more. Indeed, why should a sociologist refrain from talking when there are still unused words at his command? There is no precedent for such a procedure. What harm in substituting new words for the old as well as old words for the new? Whereupon Professor Ross proceeds to rearrange the means of control in different sequences, which he collectively calls the system of control. To those versed in the esoteric art of verbal legerdemain I will leave the task of formulating a coherent definition of social control based upon an intensive study of the work of Professor Ross which bears that title.

At the risk of imposing upon the reader's patience, I have discussed in tedious detail the theories of Spencer, Giddings, and Ross, for two reasons. In the first place, these are the only sociologists who have used the term social control to any great extent; in the second place, it was necessary, in order to answer the questions put at the beginning of this paper, that the phenomena described by that term should be clearly in mind. Before answering the questions, however, it remains to touch very briefly upon two other theories in which the term social control is not employed but in which the phenomena described are practically identical with, or definitely related to, those phenomena treated under that term in the works of the three sociologists aforementioned. In as few words as possible we will attempt to summarize the conceptions of Gumplowicz and Ward.

Gumplowicz explains control not in terms of fear but in terms of power. He derives his theory of social control from the conflict of groups and the mere brute power and authority wielded by the conqueror group over the conquered group. We may therefore summarize his theory in a definition: Social control is the power of one social group to compel the obedience of another social group.

For Lester Ward the problem is not the control of man by man but the control by man of the social forces. The "group sentiment of safety" arising from the psychic power to distinguish between pain and pleasure enabled man to avoid the self-destruction which threatened him through the subordination of ends to means. This group sentiment of safety is a rudimentary form of reason. By it man was enabled to control and utilize the social energies. It is the most fundamental of all human institutions. Out of it have emerged religion, law, morals, and all ceremonial, ecclesiastical, juridical, and political institutions. The utilization and direction of social energy by means of certain persistent social relationships growing out of the group sentiment of safety, is what Ward might have called social control.

The foregoing analyses of the various theories of social control answer the first of the questions stated at the opening of this discussion. Indulging in fleeting retrospection, we may briefly indicate the phenomena which the term "social control" has been used to describe, "or which, identical with or definitely related to the phenomena so described, have actually been otherwise described." Without attempting to assign the various meanings to their respective perpetrators, we can enumerate as follows: Social control is (1) the modification of spontaneous human conduct into definite forms of behavior as the result of the functioning of ceremonial, political, and ecclesiastical institutions; (2) the obtaining of the obedience of individuals by some sovereign power and the direction of that obedience to certain ends through the mechanism of some type of government; (3) the limiting of variation from type by social pressure; (4) the maintenance of relatively harmonious relations among individuals by the domination of the group over its component units; (5) the regulation of collective activities by the domination of the individual over the group; (6) the power of one social group to compel the obedience of another social group; (7) the utilization of social energies.

Can the term "social control" be applied with scientific precision to any or all of these phenomena? This is the second of the three questions we set out to answer. I take it that a term is "applied with scientific precision" when it is consistently used to correspond to some concrete reality directly or indirectly perceptible to the senses; and that it is otherwise used when made to correspond to things which the senses cannot perceive, or indiscriminately to different things which the senses can perceive. Stated in the parlance of common sense our second question is simply this: When we use the phrase "social control," unqualified, do we really know

[79]

what we are talking about; and if *we* do, can we expect anyone else to know? If we can't, then rather than continue to use a term so confusing, we had better, in the interests of sociology, chuck it on to the scrap heap of discarded terminology.

There may be those, however, who will still contend that the term "social control" is scientifically descriptive of a definite reality. In all of the theories analyzed above, they might say, social control has been treated as a force, a power, a means, or a something which affects human conduct in certain ways. Why not, then, synthesize the various meanings into a class term and define "social control" as the power which modifies human conduct? The facetiousness is incidental when we say that hot biscuits, mint juleps, and Welsh rarebits might each with equal reason be described as a power which modifies human conduct. Even when we qualify the word "power" with the adjectives "personal" and "social," we have done no more than enunciate the truth that certain personal and social factors affect the behavior of human beings—a truth which we can express, and better express, without enlarging the already overcrowded vocabulary of sociology. The fact that both hydrochloric and sulphuric acid will react with silver nitrate to produce a white precipitate does not lead the chemist to denominate either of these acids as the power which modifies $AgNO_3$. A disdain of the obvious impels us to refrain from pointing the moral of this analogy.

Are there phenomena of which the term "social control" is descriptive and which can be described by that term without confusion or ambiguity? This is the third and last question which we set out to answer. Obviously a term is descriptive of a phenomenon when the phenomenon is associated in the minds of most people with the term. It is thinkable that if by mutual consent the majority of English-speaking persons should suddenly begin to call the moon Clarissa, Clarissa for them the moon would become. It is superfluous to say that this is not, however, the way in which words or phrases come into use. The process is an evolutionary one. Therefore in suggesting that the term "social control" be applied to certain phenomena the study of which is within the province of sociology, we must be relatively sure that such an application will not do violence to good usage.

The word "control" has, I take it, for the majority of people, an implication more definite than the mere relationship of cause and effect. That the mutual exchange of ideas and viewpoints between two persons would not be generally spoken of as "control," is a statement doubtless not unwarranted. We would rather say that the two persons affected or influenced one another. Neither would most of us describe the phenomenon of budding

[81]

flowers as the "control" of the flowers by the rain and sun. On the other hand, if a person attempts to limit or to increase the activities of another person by appealing to his prejudices or to his morals or by any method whatsoever, we would say very naturally that *control* was being exerted. And if the horticulturist utilizes his knowledge of plant heredity to artificially select out in his roses certain characters that he wishes to cultivate, we say he *controls* the nature of his flowers. The distinction we are attempting to draw is evidently the distinction between an effect unconsciously and an effect consciously produced. By virtue of which distinction, control may be described as the attainment of a preconceived end through the conscious utilization of definite means. I am not contending that this is the only interpretation that can be or has been given to the word. I merely say that such an interpretation is consistent with good usage—perhaps more consistent than most of the meanings that have been given to the word in sociological literature.

Adhering to this distinction and interpretation, we may say that those social organizations, collectively conscious of themselves as organizations, and purposively operating to effect changes in some structure or in some persistent functioning, are organizations exercising social control. We thus understand by social control the attainment of ends through collectively conscious adaptation of means to those ends. We mean something of what Ward means by "telesis," though we prefer not to bury our meaning in polysyllabic Greek derivates. The use we here make of the term "social control" may be distinguished from other usage by the adjective "rational."

It is needless to say that the number of organizations in modern society which exercise rational social control is almost unlimited. That their variety is just as great will also be apparent upon a moment's reflection. We may have every nuance of form and function, from the gang of East-Side thugs who by certain second-story tricks make a big haul from a savings bank, to the up-to-date church that ameliorates the conditions in a poverty-stricken and crime-stained community. Government commissions, labor unions, philanthropic societies, censorship committees, the church, the press, and the state itself might all come under the category of organizations exercising rational social control. It is evident, then, that our effort to limit the application of the term "social control" amounts quantitatively to little more than a bisection of infinity. But in restricting the term to the conscious adaptation of means to end we have perhaps made a qualitative limitation that will be of service to clear thinking. Perhaps, too, our attempt to be precise, in a field where precision is so rare, is a precedent not entirely useless.

[83]

THE PROBLEM OF SOCIAL CONTROL

The study of controlling organizations is very properly within the province of sociology. The consideration of the goodness or the badness, the rightness or the wrongness, of the ends for which such organizations operate is a problem for the moralist. The function of science is of necessity descriptive and analytical, not didactic or ethical. From this standpoint, sociology is unconcerned with the formulation of positive programs of rational social control directed towards the achievement of ends which most people would evaluate "good." In another sense, however, it is concerned with such programs. It must furnish the theoretical generalizations upon which these programs are based. And I take it to be a safe prophecy that sociology will stand or fall according to whether or not its generalizations prove valid when practically applied.

"Good" and "bad" are chameleon-like words, and except in the untutored estimation of one Billy Sunday, humanity and the conditions under which humanity exists are not wholly black nor purely white. And yet despite the limitations imposed upon logical thought and sane prevision by the relativity of all things, there are certain states of existence, certain relationships between man and his environment and man and his fellow man which most people would agree were worth striving for. Is the effort to attain these desired ends always to be in vain? Sociology reveals the existence of certain factors and forces which condition social organization and the lives of human beings. Can these factors and forces be directed towards desired ends by mankind collectively organized? An affirmative answer to this question involves no philosophical assumptions concerning the doctrines of free will and determinism. When a body of physicians, by means of an antitoxin, stay the ravages of a diphtheria epidemic, who cares whether the doctors or the patients are mere "pawns on the chessboard of fate" or free agents subject only to the caprices of the Deity? The fact of significance is that, to all intents and purposes, a deadly disease has been controlled.

In the existence of a vast number of organizations rationally directing social forces to achieve definite ends, is found the refutation of the doctrine of *laissez faire*. It is not necessary that the elimination of poverty, crime, pauperism, disease, and idiocy nor that the positive development of human personality be left to the unguided redistributions of matter and motion. It is not necessary that we should periodically witness the spectacle of so-called civilized nations engaged in wholesale murder. If sociology is in truth a science, if it can factorize the social process, then it is thinkable that, through the coordination of agencies exercising rational social control, society may be changed from a gigantic coalition for the perpetuation of mediocrity into an efficient machine, intellectually directed towards the achievement of those collective hopes which are spun from the fibers of humanity's finest memories.

THE CULTURE-AREA CONCEPT

If one admits, as all scientifically minded persons must, that the classification of cultural data is prerequisite to valid factorization, two questions immediately present themselves: What is to be the unit of investigation? and What should be the basic principle of classification? Presumptive answers to these questions are quite worthless. Only by an empirical study of the artifacts, the symbols, and the traditional procedures which constitute objectively the cultures of various peoples, can the unit of investigation and the principle of classification be determined. The culture area is a conceptual by-product, so to speak, of a generation or more of inductive ethnological research. It is an empirical grouping of cultural data in which the unit of investigation and the principle of classification have been derived from direct observation of the facts and of their temporal and spatial distributions. Because the culture area is, as Kroeber has said,[1] "a non-philosophical, inductive, mainly unimpeachable organization of phenomena analogous to the 'natural' classification of animals and plants on which systematic biology rests," it is receiving more and more

[1] *Anthropology,* p. 336.

attention from sociologists who are less interested in
the chauvinistic defense of some sociological system
than in a truly scientific analysis of collective human
behavior.[2]

While the culture-area concept developed chiefly in
America and has been used, for the most part, in the
study of the American Indian, it was anticipated many
years ago in the "geographical provinces" of Adolph
Bastian.[3] Bastian, after a series of travels among the
primitive tribes of America, Africa, India, Eastern Asia,
and the islands of the South Seas, became convinced of
what in current ethnological and sociological circles is
called the "psychic unity of mankind." The fundamental similarity of the various groups composing the species *Homo sapiens,* Bastian attributed to the *Elementargedanken,* elemental ideas, with which, presumably, all
humans are blessed at birth. Nowhere in his voluminous
writings can one find a clear-cut statement of what,
specifically, elemental ideas are, but probably the most
appropriate current psychological label would be "the
original nature of man."[4] But granting the fundamental unity of the human species, how explain the amazing

[2] Cf. Herskovits and Willey, "The Cultural Approach to Sociology,"
Amer. Journ. of Soc., Vol. XXIX, September, 1923, pp. 188-199.

[3] *Der Völkergedanke, passim.* Cf. his *Ethnische Elementargedanken.*
Cf. also A. A. Goldenweiser, "Cultural Anthropology," in *The History
and Prospects of the Social Sciences* (H. E. Barnes, Ed.), p. 211.

[4] Cf. Goldenweiser, *ibid.,* p. 211.

diversity of opinion and practice which confronts the comparative ethnologist? The *Elementargedanken*, says Bastian, are transformed into *Völkergedanken*, folk ideas, by the pressure of geographical circumstances and the cultural and psychological interchanges attendant upon tribal contacts. These concretings of the abstract *Elementargedanken* occur at specific times and places. Thus result those culturally characteristic areas which Bastian called "geographical provinces." While the historian of thought will probably find in these geographical provinces a "foreshadowing" of the culture-area concept, the scientific student of society will be chiefly impressed by the vagueness of Bastian's ideas, his metaphysical leanings, the uselessness of his undefined terms, and his failure to delimit the provinces about which he was so garrulous. As Goldenweiser says,[5] Bastian's theories "proved of little practical use in the early growth of the science of man, and in due time were forgotten."

Several decades after Bastian's ponderous tomes had passed into not unmerited desuetude, Graebner, another German anthropologist, building upon the foundations laid by Ratzel, formulated the concept of the *Kulturkreis*. The *Kulturkreis* is, literally, a culture area, but the facts and theoretical presuppositions upon which it is based conspicuously differentiate it from the analogous

[5] "Diffusionism and the American School of Historical Ethnology." *Amer. Journ. of Soc.*, Vol. XXXI, July, 1925, p. 34.

concept of contemporary American ethnologists and call for exposition and critical analysis.[6]

It requires only a cursory reading of Graebner's books and monographs to realize that he is less interested in an empirical classification of cultural data than in upholding the tenets of diffusionism. To Graebner man's power to invent either artifacts or ideas is an almost negligible factor in the growth of culture, and the last inference one should draw from similar cultural features is that they were independently invented. Independent origin, indeed, can only be assumed after tribal contacts and culture-borrowing have been excluded. By thus following the logical methods of a lawyer for the defense, Graebner reached the conclusion that the central prob-

[6] For the principles and methods of Graebner and his loyal disciples, see F. Graebner, *Methode der Ethnologie*, especially pp. 125-151; "Kulturkreise und Kulturschichten in Ozeania," *Zeitschrift für Ethnologie*, Vol. XXXVII, pp. 28-54; "Die melanesische Bogenkultur und ihre Verwandten," *Anthropos*, Vol. IV, pp. 726-780, 998-1032; B. Ankermann, "Kulturkreise and Kulturschichten in Afrika," *Zeitschrift für Ethnologie*, Vol. XXXVII, pp. 54-84; W. Schmidt, "Kulturkreise und Kulturschichten in Südamerika," *Zeitschrift für Ethnologie,* Vol. XLV, pp. 1014-1124. For critical analysis of the principles and methods of the Graebnerian school, see F. Boas, review of Graebner's *Methode der Ethnologie, Science,* Vol. XXXIV, (n.s., 1911), pp. 804-810; R. H. Lowie, "On the Principle of Convergence in Ethnology," *Journal of American Folklore,* Vol. XXV, pp. 24-42; A. A. Goldenweiser, "The Principle of Limited Possibilities in the Development of Culture," *Journal of American Folklore,* Vol. XXVI, pp. 259-290; M. J. Herskovits, "The Cattle Complex in East Africa," *American Anthropologist,* Vol. XXVIII, pp. 231-239.

lem of ethnology is to give time-perspective to primitive culture, that is, to reconstruct the history of peoples who have no written records.[7]

Whether or not this be the central problem of ethnology, it necessitates a thoroughgoing study of cultural similarities, their provenience and their geographic distribution. To this task Graebner addressed himself with less of scientific cautiousness than of diffusionistic zeal. He posited two criteria to determine the degree of similarity among cultural elements, one qualitative, the criterion of form, the other quantitative. The former refers to similarities in the shape, size, color, decorative designs, etc., of two artifacts, or to observable similarities in religious rituals or social groupings; the latter, to the number of such "qualitative" resemblances.[8] Graebner seems blissfully unaware both of the identity, for all practical purposes, of his two criteria and of the limited possibilities in cultural development.[9] The closer the resemblance between two culture elements, judged by

[7] *Methode der Ethnologie*, pp. 140 ff. Cf. A. A. Goldenweiser, "Cultural Anthropology," in *The History and Prospects of the Social Sciences*, p. 235.

[8] *Methode der Ethnologie*, pp. 104 ff.

[9] Cf. M. J. Herskovits, "The Cattle Complex in East Africa," *American Anthropologist*, Vol. XXVIII, pp. 235-236; A. A. Goldenweiser, "The Principle of Limited Possibilities in the Development of Culture," *Journal of American Folklore*, Vol. XXVI, pp. 259 ff.; F. Boas, review of Graebner's *Methode der Ethnologie*, *Science*, Vol. XXXIV, n.s., pp. 804 ff.

these relatively unanalyzed criteria, the higher the probability, according to Graebner, of their common origin and of their diffusion through tribal contacts. Indeed "probability" is too mild a word, for Graebner would claim absolute validity for his criteria and, once cultural similarity has been thereby established, the common origin and diffusion of the compared elements become Graebnerian certainties, regardless of the distance between the areas where the elements are found.[10]

But Graebner does not delimit his *Kulturkreise* by mapping the geographic distributions of independent culture elements. On the contrary, he emphatically asserts that a culture element, be it an artifact, a symbol, a ritual, a social grouping, has no independent existence and never travels alone.[11] It is an inseparable part of a cluster of culture elements which constitute a unity, stabilized in a given area and diffused as a whole.[12]

[10] Graebner, *op. cit.*, pp. 62 ff.

[11] Graebner, *op. cit.*, pp. 115 ff.

[12] Graebner's dogmatic assertion that a culture trait is never singly diffused, but always as a unit in a *Kulturkomplex*, is one of the most palpable absurdities in ethnological literature. It can best be described in Graebner's own phrase, *kulturgeschichtliches Nonsens*. For an excellent illustration of the independent dissemination of culture traits and of their fortuitous coalescence into tribal complexes, see R. F. Benedict, "The Concept of the Guardian Spirit in North America," *Memoirs* of the American Anthropological Association, No. 29, especially pp. 84-85. Cf. R. H. Lowie, *Primitive Society*, Chap. XV; E. Sapir, "Time Perspective in Aboriginal American Culture," *Memoir 90*, Canada Department of Mines, Geological Survey, pp. 44-51.

THE CULTURE-AREA CONCEPT

This cluster, or group of adhesive cultural features, to use Tylor's phrase, is the Graebnerian *Kulturkomplex*, and the criteria of similarity noted above are applied to culture elements only for the purpose of establishing the empirical and logical identity of various culture complexes. The *Kulturkreis* does not presuppose absolute unity of cultural conditions nor absolute continuity in the dissemination of culture elements, for the possibility of cultural stratification must always be taken into account. It is based upon the simple fact, says Graebner, "dass ein bestimmter Komplex von Kulturelementen für ein bestimmtes Gebiet charakteristisch und in der Hauptsache darauf beschränkt ist." [13] A *Kulturkreis* is, in other words, the area in which one finds a Graebnerian *Kulturkomplex*.

But Graebner's *Kulturkomplex* does not bear close scientific scrutiny. It is, in the first place, composed of culture elements which have been arbitrarily selected, chiefly from the realm of material culture, and which are assumed to constitute an almost indissoluble unity, without any explanation of the basis for this association. In the second place, the Graebnerian, in comparing the component culture elements of two complexes, considers only external and formal similarity and ignores completely the social milieu in which the elements are found, the different meanings which the elements may

[13] Graebner, *op. cit.*, p. 133.

THE CULTURE-AREA CONCEPT

have in the two tribal groups, and the different uses to which they may be put.[14] This may be a legitimate procedure for those who have determined at all costs to prove the universality of diffusion, but it is not a scientific method of cultural classification.

The *Kulturkreis* is, then, a far-flung cultural district in which a number of culture elements, arbitrarily selected and adjudged similar by the criteria of quality and quantity, adhere in a characteristic *Kulturkomplex*. It is not an empirical grouping of tribal or other social units according to their objective and psychological cultural resemblances; and it should be quite clear, even from the brief exposition that has been given, that Graebner's concept of the *Kulturkreis* is based upon a number of a priori assumptions and unproved postulates and that it unmistakably reflects his diffusionistic bias.[15]

Neither the geographical provinces of Bastian nor the *Kulturkreise* of Graebner are acceptable inductions from carefully observed and adequately classified ethnic data. Even as heuristic tools they are dangerously misleading.

[14] Graebner, *op. cit.*, pp. 144-146. For a more detailed criticism of the Graebnerian *Kulturkomplex*, especially as it relates to the relative importance of diffusion and parallelism in the growth of culture, see F. Boas, review of Graebner's *Methode der Ethnologie, Science,* Vol. XXXIV, n.s., pp. 805 ff.; R. H. Lowie, "On the Principle of Convergence in Ethnology," *Journal of American Folklore,* Vol. XXV, pp. 24 ff.; M. J. Herskovits, "The Cattle Complex in East Africa," *American Anthropologist,* Vol. XXVIII, pp. 231-239.

[15] Cf. A. A. Goldenweiser, "Diffusion and the American School of Historical Ethnology," *Amer. Journ. of Soc.,* Vol. XXXI, pp. 21-23.

THE CULTURE-AREA CONCEPT

For the former are quasi-mystical and based upon obsolete psychology; while the latter rest upon logical modes of classification which ignore cultural realities.

The culture areas of American ethnologists may leave much to be desired by those who long to bring order out of the chaos of human living, but they have certainly not come out of philosophical speculation or an ill-concealed effort to substantiate a preconception by specious reasoning. They bear the unmistakable stamp of inductive research and may justly be regarded as almost inevitable by-products of ethnological fieldwork among the American Indians. For this, if for no other, reason they command the attention of those tough-minded students who hold fast to the faith that even in the social sciences observation, measurement, and classification should precede generalization. There is nothing recondite or esoteric about the culture-area idea, but to understand it clearly and to evaluate its usefulness one must trace its origin and development and acquire familiarity with the methods, the principles, and the terminology of those American ethnologists whose researches have led to its formulation.[16]

[16] For popular and semi-popular descriptions of the methods and concepts of this school of American ethnologists, see F. Boas, *The Mind of Primitive Man*; A. A. Goldenweiser, *Early Civilization*; R. H. Lowie, *Primitive Society*; A. L. Kroeber, *Anthropology*; A. M. Tozzer, *Social Origins and Social Continuities*; C. Wissler, *The American Indian*; *Man and Culture*; *The Relation of Nature to Man in Aboriginal America*; W. F. Ogburn, *Social Change*; H. E. Barnes, *The*

THE CULTURE-AREA CONCEPT

The culture-area idea had its origin, according to Goldenweiser,[17] in Professor Boas' attempt to classify and arrange the ethnographic collections of the American Museum of Natural History. He found that the specimens could be ranged in relatively homogeneous groups which corresponded to specific geographical districts, and that North American could thus be divided into areas characterized by their material culture. While this "origin" is as plausible as any that has been suggested, it is highly improbable, as Wissler has recently pointed out,[18] that the culture-area concept, either in its inception or in its present form, can be attributed to any one individual. It is a natural outgrowth of research and teaching and of the efforts of several scholars to derive methodological and interpretative principles from the descriptive monographs of specialists in American Indian cultures. The scientific study of these cultures, like the scientific study of any phenomena, necessitates

New History and the Social Studies, Chap. IV. For technical expositions and for the factual materials on which the concepts of this school are based, see the monographic studies by Boas, Lowie, Wissler, Kroeber, Goldenweiser, Benedict, Herskovits, Bogoras, Swanton, Speck, Dorsey, Goddard, Holmes, Mason, Mooney, Nelson, Radin, Sapir, Spinden, Teit, Fletcher, Waterman, etc.

[17] "Cultural Anthropology," in The History and Prospects of the Social Sciences, p. 244, footnote 72. Cf. also, by the same author, "Diffusionism and the American School of Historical Ethnology," Amer. Journ. of Soc., Vol. XXXI, pp. 34-35.

[18] "The Culture-Area Concept in Social Anthropology," Amer. Journ. of Soc., Vol. XXXII, pp. 882 ff.

an analysis of large and intricate wholes into their component parts. Such analysis by American ethnologists resulted, first of all, in the methodological concept of the culture trait.

The culture trait is a unit of tribal culture.[19] But it is not a unit in the sense in which the physicist, the chemist, or the student of electrodynamics would use that term. It is not an absolute and indivisible entity with a constant quantitative value. It is, rather, what may be called a practical or an observational unit. It is a cultural element which the ethnological field-worker sees, or thinks he sees, when he sets about to describe the social life of a primitive people. For example, among the Todas a man may not utter the name of his mother's brother.[20] This observed fact is recorded as a culture trait. A field-worker among the Blackfoot Indians notes that at certain times members of this tribe torture themselves.[21] This is a trait of the tribal culture. The Central Eskimo do their sea-hunting in kayak;[22] the Sioux Indians live in tipis;[23] a Crow Indian must not speak to

[19] C. Wissler, *Man and Culture*, p. 50.

[20] W. H. R. Rivers, *The Todas*, p. 626.

[21] L. Spier, "The Sun Dance of the Plains Indians," *Anthropological Papers*, American Museum of Natural History, Vol. XVI, part VII, p. 461.

[22] F. Boas, "The Central Eskimo," *Sixth Annual Report*, Bureau of Ethnology, p. 486.

[23] C. Wissler, *The Relation of Nature to Man in Aboriginal America*, p. 1.

his wife's parents.[24] These are randomly selected illustrations of culture traits.

In the earlier stages of anthropological development in this country, the ideal of the field-worker was to describe completely, and as objectively and concretely as possible, not only all of the material and non-material culture traits of a tribe but also its language and its racial characteristics. But life is short and time is fleeting, and American anthropologists soon realized that this ideal exceeded the grasp of a single individual. Specialization followed along three chief lines: linguistics, somatology, and culture.[25] Nor was division of labor to stop here. The complete description of the culture traits of one tribe is a big task; of several tribes, well-nigh impossible.[26] American ethnologists therefore came to concentrate upon single tribes or upon several neighboring tribes with similar cultures. Specialization became not only topical but regional.[27] The point to be noted here is that the attempt to describe

[24] R. H. Lowie, *Primitive Society*, p. 87.

[25] Cf. C. Wissler, "Recent Developments in Anthropology," in *Recent Developments in the Social Sciences* (E. C. Hayes, Ed.), pp. 57 ff.

[26] For an interesting list of data "needed to characterize the material culture of an American tribe," see C. Wissler, "Material Culture of the North American Indians," *American Anthropologist*, Vol. XVI, No. 3 (n.s.), pp. 448-449.

[27] Cf. C. Wissler, "The Culture-Area Concept in Social Anthropology," *Amer. Journ. of Soc.*, Vol. XXXII, pp. 882 ff.

THE CULTURE-AREA CONCEPT

completely the culture traits of the American Indian literally forced ethnologists into specialization by geographical areas. The boundaries to these areas, as Wissler points out,[28] were not absolutely set by the investigators but were inherent in the phenomena themselves. As soon as comparisons were made of the findings of these various regional specialists, the culture-area concept became practically inevitable.

Further analysis of the culture trait brought out two points which receive emphasis in current ethnological literature. The first is that the culture traits of different tribes should never be identified merely on the basis of their objective similarity; they must also be psychologically similar, that is, they must have the same "meaning" in the tribes in which they are found. It is here that the American school takes definite issue with the Graebnerians, who, as we have seen,[29] contend that objective resemblance between two culture elements establishes identity and proves diffusion from a common source. Boas has tersely expressed the contrary position of American ethnologists as follows:

The concepts of comparability and homogeneity . . . have to deal not only with historical relationships, but . . . with psychological similarity. . . . If the aged are killed by one people for economic reasons, by another to insure them

[28] *Ibid.*, p. 883.
[29] *Supra*, pp. 94-95.

a happy future life, then the two customs are not comparable, even if they should have their origin in the same historical sources.[30]

The second fact revealed by a scrutiny of the culture trait is that it is "not a clear-cut unit, but a kind of complex." [31] For example, the trait of Toda culture mentioned above,[32] that a man may not utter the name of his mother's brother, does not stand isolated from all other Toda traits. On the contrary, it is, from the Toda point of view, inextricably bound up, logically and functionally, with a number of other traits. It is a link in a series which cuts across Toda social organization, Toda etiquette, and Toda religion. Or to cite Wissler's frequently quoted illustration, taken from Jenks's monograph, the Ojibway Indians use wild rice for food. This is a trait of Ojibway culture. But, as Wissler says:

. . . each member of the tribe did not snatch his rice food directly from the plant as do the birds, but received it as the end of a cycle of activities in which he, as an individual, played a varying part. Thus, though the plant is wild, some care was given the plots where it grew; later, the plants were tied in bunches to discourage rice-eating birds, then the rice was gathered, cured, hulled, winnowed, stored, cooked, and eaten. . . . The many processes involved required techniques of various complexities and special appli-

[30] F. Boas, review of Graebner's *Methode der Ethnologie, Science,* Vol. XXXIV, n.s., p. 808.
[31] Wissler, *Man and Culture,* p. 51.
[32] *Supra,* p. 97.

[100]

ances. But that is not all, for intimately bound up in the whole are property rights, labor obligations, etiquette, methods of keeping time, and a number of special religious observances, prohibitions, and taboos.[33]

Some of the traits in a complex are, obviously, necessarily related to each other. Prerequisite to the Toda taboo on uttering the name of one's maternal uncle is a classificatory system which makes certain distinctions in kinship by blood and marriage. An Ojibway Indian cannot eat wild rice until it has been gathered. The relations between such traits are functional and necessary. But other traits in a complex are not necessarily related to each other. While from the Ojibway point of view the gathering of wild rice may be a no more "necessary" preliminary for eating it than the performance of a religious ritual, it is quite clear that the latter trait could be omitted without disturbing the remainder of the complex.[34] A culture complex is, then, a cluster of culture traits some of which are functionally associated and therefore indispensable, others of which are apparently related only fortuitously, but all of which are knit together into what seems to the members of the tribe possessing the complex, a logical whole. It should

[33] Wissler, *op. cit.*, pp. 51-52. Cf. A. E. Jenks, "The Wild Rice Gatherers of the Upper Lakes," *Nineteenth Annual Report*, Bureau of American Ethnology, Part II.
[34] Wissler, *op. cit.*, p. 64.

be noted that the culture complex as thus described differs markedly from the Graebnerian *Kulturkomplex*. The latter, as we have seen,[35] is a group of arbitrarily selected culture elements, chiefly artifacts, assumed to constitute an indivisible unity which is diffused as a whole; the former is simply a description of the interrelation and interdependence of a number of observed traits, material and non-material, with no assumptions as to the origin and diffusion of these traits, either singly or in combination.

When one traces the distribution of a trait complex over a wide area, such as a continent, it quickly becomes apparent that the complex is not a constant, having the same form and content wherever found, but a variable. Not only do individual traits differ, in practice, from one social group to another within a given tribe, but the complex as a whole varies from one tribe to another. The so-called "maize complex," for example, is widely distributed among North American Indian tribes.[36] It includes all the practices, processes, and ceremonies which accompany the production of maize and its use as a staple food. But the methods of planting, cultivating, gathering, grinding, etc., and the ceremonial and ideology associated with these procedures, exhibit tribal variations. Some of the processes may be alto-

[35] *Supra*, p. 93.
[36] Wissler, *The American Indian*, p. 20.

gether omitted; others may be highly elaborated in one tribe and extremely attenuated in another. The sun dance, a ceremonial complex found among the Plains Indians, is composed, according to Professor Spier,[37] of eighty-two traits or elements. But no one tribe has all these traits; the number varies from five in the Canadian Dakota tribe to fifty-four in the Arapaho. It is not difficult, however, for the trained investigator to find among these differences the typical or modal trait and the typical complex, and to recognize the variations as deviations from these norms.[38] A glance at Wissler's map showing the distribution of the Plains type of female dress,[39] will make clear that the local differences are merely variations on the same stylistic theme. A culture complex may, in the light of the foregoing, be redefined as a varying cluster of culture traits, each of which is itself a variable.

If the geographic distribution of a culture complex be plotted on a map, the complex and its variants will not be randomly scattered, but definitely localized in a continuous area. Wissler has shown this to be true for practically all the major trait complexes of the American Indians.[40] It also appears that if we select the most highly

[37] Cited by Wissler in *The Relation of Nature to Man in Aboriginal America*, pp. 83 ff.
[38] Wissler, *Man and Culture*, p. 53.
[39] *Ibid.*, p. 54.
[40] Wissler, *The American Indian, passim*.

elaborated variant of a complex, that is, the one composed of the largest number of interdependent traits, it will be found to occupy a "central" position in relation to the other variants. The contiguous variants will most closely resemble the "typical" or "central" complex, in the number of constituent traits and the intricateness of their interrelation, and this similarity will decrease as the distance from the "center" increases. Wissler holds that all trait complexes thus far studied fall into these zoned distributions around common centers.[41]

What happens, one may ask, when the geographic distributions of many trait complexes are superimposed? As ethnologists have repeatedly demonstrated, from Tylor's pioneer investigation [42] to the recent study by Hobhouse, Wheeler, and Ginsberg,[43] trait complexes coincide, they are associated and integrated in characteristic clusters, they accumulate in a circumscribed territory. The relation between coincident trait complexes does not seem to be a functional or necessary one. In fact, the contrary has repeatedly been demonstrated, as in the well-known association between the maize com-

[41] Wissler, *The Relation of Nature to Man in Aboriginal America*, pp. 180-182 and *passim*.

[42] E. B. Taylor, "On a Method of Investigating the Development of Institutions; applied to Laws of Marriage and Descent," *Journal of the Anthropological Institute of Great Britain and Ireland*, Vol. XVIII, pp. 245-272.

[43] Hobhouse, Wheeler, and Ginsburg, *The Material Culture and Social Institutions of the Simpler Peoples*.

plex and the pottery complex in North America. Trait complexes are found together for the most part simply because historical causes have brought them together.[44] We are not here primarily concerned with the basis of this association, but with the observable fact.

If now, to follow Wissler's lead once more, we consider all trait complexes jointly, and shift the point of view from the cultural units, namely, the trait and the complex, to the social units, it will be found that these social units, namely, the tribes, can be ranged in relatively homogeneous groups localized in continuous areas. "This will give us culture areas, or a classification of social groups according to their cultural traits."[45] Except in dealing with archaeological data, it is difficult and perhaps unnecessary to maintain the distinction between a cultural unit and a social unit, for culture traits and culture complexes are after all merely the folkways and mores of living tribes.

The exposition up to this point should have made it fairly clear that a culture area is not a rigidly delimited district. Its periphery is always, to some extent, arbitrary. The intersecting straight lines which mark off, for example,[46] the Plains Indian culture area could be shifted here and there into a somewhat different geo-

[44] Wissler, The American Indian, pp. 385-388.
[45] Ibid., p. 218.
[46] Ibid., p. 221.

metric design without doing violence to the assembled data or to the principle of classification. Indeed the boundary lines of a culture area are hardly more than a graphic device to indicate that within the enclosed region there is a cluster of trait complexes in characteristic combination, or, to phrase it from the viewpoint of the social units, that the flexible periphery encompasses a group of tribes whose culture is relatively homogeneous. The culture-area concept is empirical and analytical, and it should always be understood that further research may necessitate expansion or reduction of a given area. Occasionally, of course, the boundary line to an area may be set by climatic or other geographical conditions, as Herskovits found in his study of the culture areas of Africa, where the line of sixty-inch rainfall unequivocally divides the Congo area from the East African Cattle Area,[47] but this is exceptional.

It should also be clear from the foregoing exposition that the tribes included in a culture area are not thus grouped as culturally homogeneous merely because they objectively exhibit similar trait complexes. The social attitudes accompanying these trait complexes, the social emphasis given to one complex rather than another, the way in which the trait complexes interpenetrate to form a characteristic cultural pattern, must all be considered.

[47] M. J. Herskovits, "A Preliminary Consideration of the Culture Areas of Africa," *American Anthropologist*, Vol. XXVI, p. 52.

THE CULTURE-AREA CONCEPT

For this reason the culture-area concept is said to be not only objective but psychological.[48] For this, and for other reasons, it stands out in sharp contrast to the Graebnerian *Kulturkreis.*[49]

Since, as we have seen,[50] a "typical" trait complex and its variants fall into a zoned geographic distribution around a common center, it is to be expected that a number of coincident trait complexes will have the same distribution form. Now a tribal culture is composed of coincident trait complexes integrated, objectively and psychologically, in a characteristic way. It follows, then, that the tribal cultures within a given culture area must be regarded as variants around a "type" or norm and that they will be distributed geographically like trait complexes. This expectation is realized in the facts. The Plains Indian culture area will serve as an illustration. Wissler describes the type of culture in this area as follows:

The chief traits of this culture are dependence upon the buffalo or bison, and the very limited use of roots and berries; absence of fishing; lack of agriculture; the tipi as a movable dwelling; transportation by land only, with the dog and the travois (in historic times with the horse); want of basketry and pottery; no true weaving; clothing of buffalo

[48] Cf. A. A. Goldenweiser, "Cultural Anthropology," in *The History and Prospects of the Social Sciences* (H. E. Barnes, Ed.), p. 244.

[49] *Supra,* pp. 89-94.

[50] *Supra,* p. 104.

[107]

and deer skins; a special bead technique; high development of work in skins; special rawhide work (parfleche, cylindrical bag, etc.); use of a circular shield; weak development of work in wood, stone, and bone. Their art is strongly geometric, but as a whole, not symbolic; social organization tends to the simple band; a camp circle organization; a series of societies for men; sun-dance ceremony; sweat-house observances, scalp dances, etc.[51]

The constituent trait complexes of this culture are not spread uniformly over the area. Some of the tribes have all of the trait complexes, highly elaborated; others have nearly all; others have relatively few of the positive trait complexes and a number of the negative ones; while still others have a preponderance of the negative complexes. To put it more generally, any given tribe in this area is, in certain respects, like every other tribe in the area; in other respects, it is like the tribes in a restricted part of the area; in still others, it is unique.[52] If the thirty-one Plains Indian tribes be classified according to the number of trait complexes, characteristic of this area, which they exhibit, and according to the elaborateness of these complexes,[53] several groupings emerge: (1) a group of eleven tribes—the Assiniboin, Arapaho, Blackfoot, Cheyenne, Comanche, Crow, Gros Ventre,

[51] Wissler, *op. cit.*, pp. 218 and 220.
[52] Cf. A. A. Goldenweiser, *Early Civilization*, p. 123.
[53] "Elaborateness" refers chiefly to the number of culture traits composing the complex.

Kiowa, Kiowa-Apache, Sarsi, and Teton-Dakota—having all the chief culture traits of the area; (2) a group of about seventeen tribes—Arikara, Mandan, Shoshoni, Osage, Wichita, etc.—having most of the positive traits and some of the negative ones, such as a limited use of pottery and basketry or less dependence upon the buffalo and more upon deer and small game; (3) a group having a high percentage of Plains traits but, in addition, many traits not characteristic of this area.[54] A study of the map will show that the tribes composing the first group are contiguous from north to south and occupy the heart of the Plains area; that the second group divides geographically into two groups, one located on the eastern border of the central group, the other on the western border; and that the tribes composing the third group are nearest the boundaries of the Plains area, farthest, that is, from the central tribes. The habitat of this central group is called the culture center and its culture is taken "as the type for the area as a whole." As we move from this center we find tribal variations from this type increasing, not abruptly but gradually, until we come to regions where the tribal cultures exhibit many extraneous elements. These outlying districts are called marginal areas. The justification for the use of this term is found in the fact that the "extraneous elements" are seen, upon investigation, to be "typical"

[54] Wissler, *op. cit.*, pp. 220-222, especially Fig. 59.

[109]

of other culture areas. That is, if we continued to move, say westward, from the central tribes of the Plains, we should encounter more and more extraneous elements until eventually we should come upon a cluster of tribal cultures whose coincident trait complexes constituted a distinct type. The habitat of these tribes would be the culture center of the Plateau area.

Exposition in terms of a single illustration has the disadvantage of seeming to posit unproved assumptions. Culture areas are not data but inductions. When the culture of a large portion of the earth's surface, such as a continent, is minutely analyzed, intensively studied and geographically distributed, it is found that trait complexes coincide in specific regions in characteristic combinations and that the inhabiting tribes are culturally homogeneous, that is, they have about the same trait complexes and the complexes are made up of about the same traits. Such regions are culture centers. They are the nuclei, so to speak, of culture areas, which may be regarded as types of culture plus their variants. Obviously in all culture areas will be found districts in which the tribal cultures are of doubtful classification. These are the marginal areas.

The foregoing exposition of the culture area and its subsidiary concepts may now be briefly resumed. The culture area is, first of all, and, for the purpose of this essay, most important of all, a method of cultural classification. It does not presuppose a diffusionistic theory nor is it based upon any assumptions save the methodological assumptions that culture is classifiable and that the mode of classification should be dictated by cultural realities. It developed naturally along with that specialization in anthropological research which led field-workers to concentrate upon one or two tribal cultures and eventually, through comparison of the resulting monographs, to discover that all specific social procedures in aboriginal North America were regional rather than tribal. The delimitation of culture areas involves an analysis of artifacts, folkways, customs, and institutions into their constituent elements. The simplest observational unit revealed by such analysis is called a culture trait; but scrutiny of the culture trait shows that it is not an isolable entity but a link in a series of functionally and fortuitously interrelated traits. This concatenation of traits, or cycle of unit-processes, is called a culture complex or a trait complex. Trait complexes are classified according to their objective and psychological similarities, and their geographic distributions plotted. It is thereby discovered that trait complexes are not randomly scattered but that they tend to coincide, to accumulate in various places in characteristic combinations. Such coincidences of trait complexes determine the loci of culture areas. Description in terms of the trait complex, the cultural unit, tends to emphasize the fact that cultural similarities cut across political, that is, tribal, lines, but the culture area is more realistically described in terms of the social unit. From this point of view the culture area is simply an empirical geographic grouping of tribes having similar cultures. But similarity, in the parlance of American ethnologists, is not identity. A culture area merely defines geographically a type of culture and its variants. Within it one finds a centrally located group of tribes whose culture is highly homogeneous. The habitat of these tribes is the culture center. Surrounding this center are other tribes whose culture is less homogeneous but obviously a variation from the central culture. Surrounding these, farthest from the center, are tribes whose culture is still less homogeneous and in many features quite different from the central culture. The habitats of these tribes are the marginal areas. The boundaries of culture areas are therefore merely diagrammatic, serving to differentiate culture centers and to mark roughly the geographic limits of variation from these norms.

Culture areas, as thus conceived, have been established with varying degrees of exactitude for North and South America and for Africa. Ten North American areas are recognized: Plains, Plateau, California, North Pacific Coast, Eskimo, Mackenzie, Eastern Woodland, Southeastern, Southwestern, Nahua.[55] These areas are the

[55] Wissler, *op. cit.,* pp. 218 ff.

gradual and empirical results of intensive fieldwork and research. With the exception of the Plateau and Mackenzie areas, both of which are vague in positive trait complexes, the distinctness and approximate boundaries of these culture areas have been clearly established. They represent, as Kroeber says,

a consensus of opinion as to the classification of a mass of facts, slowly arrived at, contributed to by many workers, probably accepted in exact identity by no two of them, but in essential outlines by all.[56]

The five South American areas—Chibcha, Inca, Guanaco, Amazon, Antillean [57]—are products of less intensive research, and future studies will doubtless increase the number.[58] Herskovits has mapped the East African Cattle Area [59] and laid the foundations for a mapping of other African areas,[60] but his work must be regarded as preliminary to the precise delimitation of culture areas for this continent.

The culture-area concept has been used extensively by American ethnologists in the study of diffusion. While the geographically continuous distribution of cultural

[56] Kroeber, *Anthropology*, p. 336.
[57] Wissler, *op. cit.*, pp. 245 ff.
[58] Kroeber, *op. cit.*, p. 337.
[59] Herskovits, "The Cattle Complex in East Africa," *American Anthropologist*, Vol. XXVIII.
[60] Herskovits, "A Preliminary Consideration of the Culture Areas of Africa," *American Anthropologist*, Vol. XXVI, pp. 50-63.

similarities is doubtless best explained by diffusion from common centers of dispersal, it should be understood that this is an inference from the classified data, not an assumption, as in the case of the Graebnerian *Kultur-kreis,* upon which the classification depends for its validity. The culture area has no time-depth,[61] and though it has proved to be a valuable heuristic tool in making historical reconstructions, it is primarily a descriptive, not an historical, concept.[62] Neither should the implications of environmental determinism conveyed by the term "culture area" be taken literally. Whatever, and to what extent, geographic factors determine culture areas is a research problem, not a postulate upon which the culture-area concept is based. In brief, the culture area is a classification of coexistential cultural data according to their objective and psychological resemblances and in terms of their regional distributions. It represents an attempt to reduce the chaotic details of primitive social behavior to the level of human comprehension, to provide that ordered body of knowledge without which scientific factorization and generalization are impossible.

While the culture-area concept has been, up to now, used chiefly by the ethnologists in the study of the simpler peoples, it is receiving more and more atten-

[61] Herskovits, *op. cit.,* p. 657.

[62] Sapir, "Time Perspective in Aboriginal American Culture," Canada Department of Mines, Geological Survey, *Memoir 90* Anthropological Series, No. 13, pp. 44 ff.

tion from sociologists and other social scientists,[63] who recognize the applicability of this mode of classification to the culture of civilized societies. A number of questions immediately arise: What are the culture areas of modern society? What data are available for their delimitation? Will the geographic distribution of the trait complexes of western and oriental civilizations give districts of sufficient homogeneity to be of service to the sociologist? If not, what other regional characterizations are necessary?

[63] Cf., F. H. Giddings, *The Scientific Study of Human Society*, p. 16; S. A. Rice, *Farmers and Workers in American Politics*, pp. 177 ff.; M. M. Willey, "Society and Its Cultural Heritage," in *An Introduction to Sociology*, by Davis, Barnes, and others, pp. 495-587; C. Wissler, *Man and Culture*, Chap. II and *passim;* "The Culture Concept in Social Anthropology," *loc. cit.*, pp. 881 ff.; A. A. Goldenweiser, "Diffusionism and the American School of Historical Ethnology," *loc. cit.*, p. 37.

FRATERNITY

It is, I suppose, a symptom of age that I have less and less aversion to moralizing. An unwilling exile from the scarlet halls of youth, I find myself more and more concerned with the philosophy of life and less with the actual business of living. In the years since I passed from these academic shades into the white light of Forty-second and Broadway, I have thought much about the larger and more fundamental meanings of fraternity life. The more I think of it, the more convinced I am that the motto of ΦΓΔ epitomizes all that is finest and best in the human struggle for survival and advantage.

It has become a commonplace of social science that there never has been and probably never will be any such thing as individual existence. That no man liveth to himself alone has become a scientific truth. Nature has seen fit to distribute irregularly her life-sustaining wares, and the necessity of group life—of collective effort —is inherent in the very nature of the planet on which we dwell. But within those larger groupings due to environmental pressure are smaller groups of far greater significance. They are variously motivated—by perceptions of utility, by instinct, by economic interests. But

FRATERNITY

perhaps the greatest group-forming factor in society is
the recognition by intelligent human beings that there
are other human beings like themselves in traditions,
beliefs, aspirations, and ideals. It is such a social force
that makes a fraternity. It is no spirit of exclusiveness;
no lofty assumption of superiority—simply a conviction
that mental and moral likeness is the basis of a pleasur-
able and profitable union. And the bond which holds
together and perpetuates such a group is that which we
designate by the first Greek letter of our motto and
which reverently we name friendship.

But friendship if regarded as an end in itself becomes
all too often a silly and a futile thing. Fine as are its
joys and sweet as are its consolations, the ultimate measure of its worth must be sought in the ends it helps us
to attain. A fraternal group that does not lift its components to some higher plane, that does not consciously
seek the realization of ideals, is worse than useless. Even
in an age when jazz music and the shimmy are regarded
as the highest expressions of the artistic impulse, the
belief still survives in progress, in the upward and
onward trend of human life. God only knows what
justifies the existence of most modern girls and women
—save of course their incubatory propensities—but there
is only one thing that can really justify the existence of
a man, and that is an unceasing effort to make some
contribution, however humble, to the world in which

[117]

he lives. Fraternal friendship should aid him in making his contribution; that indeed is its highest function. And I think this is what our founders meant when they put Delta in our motto.

But achievement through friendship, just as the utilization of any means to a given end, may degenerate into wretched Jesuitism unless we look well to the manner in which we employ the means. The rules of the game—a decent regard for the rights of others—must be observed. Our striving for achievement through friendship must be the striving of cultured men. Such thoughts, it seems to me, embody some of the deeper meanings of PGD. It is a motto that has behind it, fellows, a noble—a Grecian—philosophy of life, and it is based upon principles that have the immutability of long attested scientific laws. And yet I sometimes think that it is incomplete, that one word has been omitted. It is there, doubtless by implication, but I feel it should be explicitly stated. And that word is Fortitude.

As we contemplate the ever shifting elements of the world which lies about us, we are, I think, more and more impressed with the grim and sinister aspects of human destiny. Life is hard, it is brutal, unjust, and unmoral. You do not think so now. This is your springtime, your halcyon days. But times will come when you must sit in the sepulchres of gloom and watch your dreams go silently to dust; times when you must look upon the decayed corpses of all your illusions; times when you will realize that pain and grief and broken faith and unrequited love are not merely the imaginings of pessimistic philosophers and sentimental lady novelists, but hideous realities that may come unexpectedly and unbidden into the happiest lives. You will stand in the twilight of all your idols; you will know that divine omnipotence and divine mercy cannot be reconciled. You will lift up your eyes and your voice unto the hills and the only answer will be the echo of your wailing plea for pity. It is then that you must have recourse to that universal and unalterable faith that "Somehow far off discordant sounds are wed, somewhere far off the broken rays converge." Under the inspiration of that faith, which requires an almost divine fortitude, you will "carry on." You will believe, as others have before you, that the Promethean fire which burns in the heart of a real man cannot be extinguished by the waters of adversity. You will thrill to the revelation that pain and privation and penury are negligible, that even death is a little thing. In the blackness of the gaunt, eventual end, if you are a real Fiji, you will voice the dauntless challenge of old frosted Moses: " 'Tisn't life that matters; it's the courage you bring to it." And when you have found the strength to say that, you will stand once more in the sunshine.